LEATHERWORKING REVIVAL

LEATHER CRAFTING BOOK TO LEATHER MAINTENANCE, REPAIR AND RESTORATION

"BREATHING NEW LIFE INTO OLD LEATHER ITEMS"

Colored Interior

DR. FANATOMY

copyright@ dr. fanatomy 2024

All rights reserved. No part of this publication may be reproduced, distributed, or transmitted in any form or by any means, including photocopying, recording, or other electronic or mechanical methods, without the prior written permission of the publisher, except in the case of brief quotations embodied in critical reviews and certain other noncommercial uses permitted by copyright law.

This book is a work of non-fiction , and any resemblance to actual persons, living or dead, or actual events is purely coincidental.

The information and techniques described in this book are intended for educational and informational purposes only. The author and publisher shall not be held liable for any injury, damage, or loss arising from the use or misuse of the information presented in this book.

While every effort has been made to ensure the accuracy of the information contained within this book, the author and publisher make no warranties or representations, express or implied, about the completeness, accuracy, reliability, suitability, or availability with respect to the contents of this book for any purpose. The use of any information provided in this book is at the reader's own risk.

BONUS BOOKLET - LEATHERWORKING

Thanks for purchasing the book, and welcome to the community!
We are providing Bonus Booklet that contains :

- 10 Beginner Frequently Questions (FAQs) with answers.
- Top 10 Recommended Youtube Channels
- Patterns and Designs for a few initial projects

Click Here/copy this link: https://bit.ly/FanatomyLWBonus

Else you can scan the below barcode

TABLE OF CONTENTS

1. INTRODUCTION: MAINTAIN, REPAIR, AND RESTORE LEATHER (4-7)

   - WELCOME TO LEATHERWORKING REVIVAL: MAINTAIN, REPAIR & RESTORE
   - UNDERSTANDING THE ESSENCE OF LEATHER REPAIR AND RESTORATION OF LEATHER REPAIR AND RESTORATION
   - LEATHER DAMAGE, REPAIR, RESTORATION AND MAINTENANCE

2. LEATHER CLEANING AND CARE (8-18)

   - LEATHER TYPES AND CARE
   - CLEANING AND MAINTAINING LEATHER
   - CHOOSING THE RIGHT CLEANING PRODUCTS
   - CLEANING TECHNIQUES FOR DIFFERENT LEATHER ITEMS/PRODUCTS
   - LEATHER CLEANING GUIDELINES
   - BEST PRACTICES FOR LEATHER CLEANING AND MAINTENANCE
   - THINGS TO AVOID IN LEATHER CARE AND CLEANING OF OLD LEATHER ITEMS

3. BASICS OF LEATHER REPAIR (19-27)

   - BASICS OF LEATHER REPAIR
   - IDENTIFYING TYPES OF DAMAGE
   - LEATHER AND VINYL FURNITURE CARE TIPS

TABLE OF CONTENTS

4. BASICS OF LEATHER RESTORATION (28-33)

- DEMYSTIFYING LEATHER RESTORATION
- ASSESSING COLOR FADE AND LOSS OF LUSTER
- COMPREHENSIVE TIPS FOR LEATHER RESTORATION
- SIX STEPS FOR LEATHER RESTORATION

5. LEATHER REPAIR AND RESTORATION - DAMAGE TYPES, TOOLS, AND TECHNIQUES (34-38)

- UNDERSTANDING LEATHER DAMAGE
- LEATHER REPAIR AND RESTORATION TOOLS

6. BASIC SAFETY GUIDELINES (39-45)

- SAFETY AND FIRST AID IN LEATHERWORKING

7. LEATHER RESTORATION PROJECTS (46-75)

- RESTORING OLD LEATHER BOOTS
- FIX RIPS AND CRACKS IN YOUR LEATHER SOFA/CHAIR
- LEATHER BAG RESTORATION
- LEATHER SATCHEL RESTORATION
- FADED LEATHER JACKET RESTORATION
- LEATHER POUCH RESTORATION
- LEATHER BELT RESTORATION
- WHITE LEATHER SHOE RESTORATION
- LEATHER BRIEFCASE RESTORATION
- RESTORING A LEATHER-WRAPPED STEERING WHEEL

TABLE OF CONTENTS

8. TIPS & BEGINNER QUESTIONS (76-90)

- 20 TIPS FOR BEGINNER LEATHER RESTORATION PROJECTS
- BEGINNER QUESTIONS
- FAQ TABLE

8. APPENDIX (91-98)

- APPENDIX 1 - LEATHER SUPPLIERS
- APPENDIX 2 - YOUTUBE CHANNELS FOR LEATHER RESTORATION PROJECTS
- APPENDIX 3 - ONLINE RESOURCES
- APPENDIX 4 - GLOSSARY

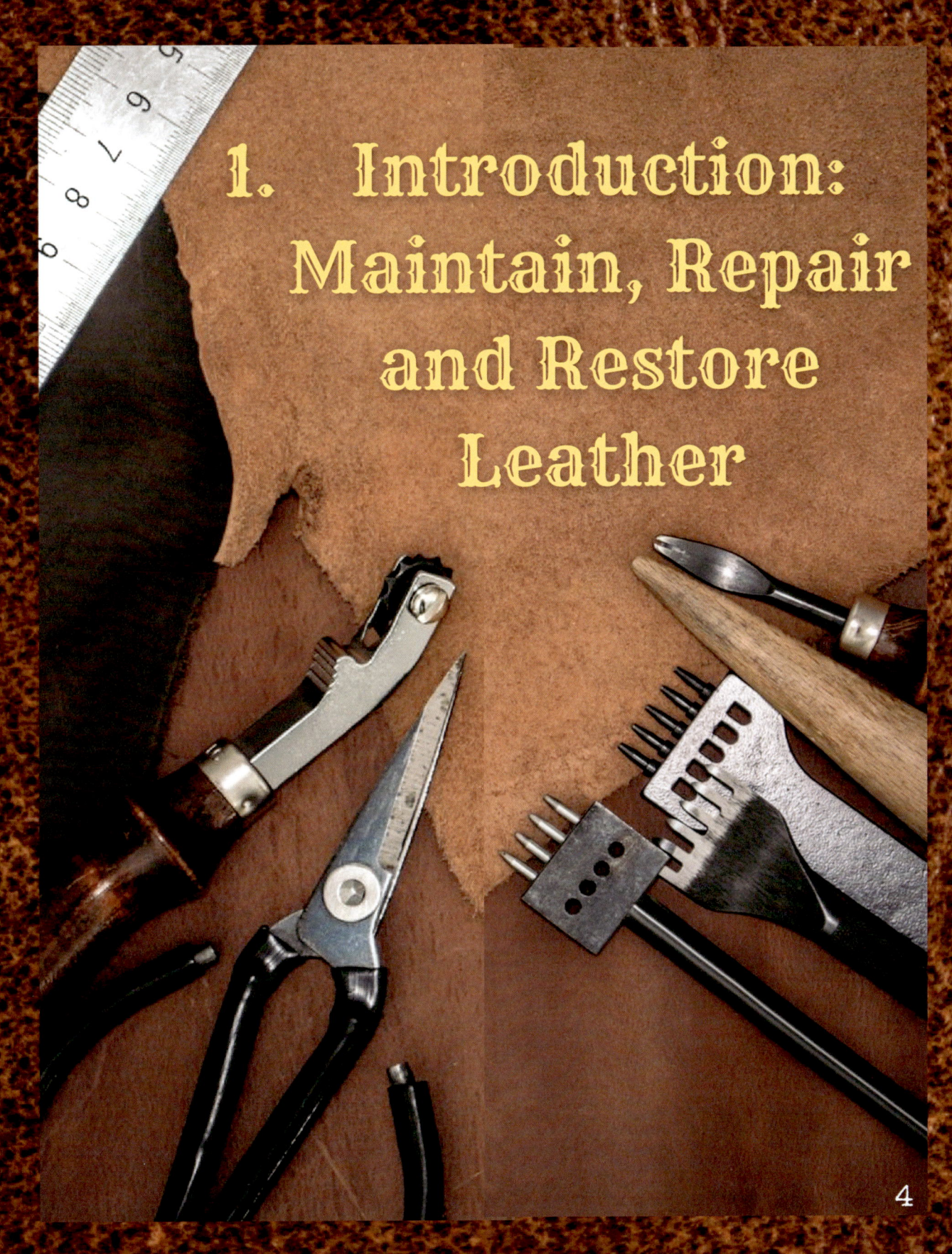

1. Introduction: Maintain, Repair and Restore Leather

Welcome to Leatherworking Revival: Maintain, repair & Restore

- Discover the secrets of repairing and restoring leather to breathe new life into cherished items with "Leatherworking Revival," your guide to the artful world of DIY leather crafting.

- This book is not just a book but an adventure. Each chapter takes you closer to mastering the craft of leather repair and restoration. Learn how to identify, assess, and repair wear and tear on leather items.

- Experience the transformative power of restoration. Witness faded colors regain their vibrancy and worn surfaces come alive. It's not just about fixing; it's about rejuvenation.

- Discover how leather crafting involves crafting narratives and preserving the legacy of each leather piece, going beyond mere mending and repair.

Understanding the Essence of Leather Repair and Restoration of Leather Repair and Restoration

In this segment, we will explore the leather repair and restoration world. We will unravel the complex layers that comprise this craft's essence. We will delve into each facet, starting from the basic concept of leather repair, progressing to the transformative artistry of leather restoration, and appreciating the interconnection between repair, restoration, and the vast world of leather crafting.

Grasping the Concept of Leather Repair

Leather repair is more than just fixing a broken item; it's about preserving the character of each leather piece. Imagine a favorite leather bag with a worn-out strap or a cherished jacket with a tear. One must recognize these imperfections and know how to fix them to understand leather repair. From patching tiny holes to stitching seams, it's a skill that allows you to revive your treasured leather possessions and give them a new life.

Unveiling the Art of Leather Restoration

Restoration is the art of revitalizing worn-out leather, Replenishing faded colors, and removing signs of aging. Think of an antique leather chair that has lost its shine or a vintage bag with faded colors. You can transform aged leather items into timeless treasures using various restoration techniques. This journey of rejuvenation involves exploring techniques beyond just repairs, allowing you to unveil the hidden beauty within each piece. Restoration is truly where the magic happens, as every step in the process reveals the allure of these items that have stood the test of time.

Connecting Repair and Restoration to Leather Crafting

Leather repair and restoration are not separate from leather crafting but rather essential components. Recognizing this connection means acknowledging that these skills are practical and creative expressions. As you become proficient in repair and restoration techniques, you can easily incorporate them into your overall repertoire of leather crafting skills.

It's important to understand that the stitches and patches you add are functional and contribute to the story behind each leather item.

Understanding the core concepts of leather repair and restoration is about acquiring skills and embracing a mindset. It's a journey where you transition from fixing to creating, from preserving to revitalizing. As we proceed through the chapters, remember that each stitch and restoration is a stroke on the canvas of your leather crafting adventure.

Leather Damage, Repair, Restoration and Maintenance

#	Description	Repair	Restoration	Maintenance
Leather Damage	Common damages include tears, scratches, and stains.	Identify the type and extent of the damage.	Assess the severity and plan a restoration approach.	Regularly clean, condition, and protect.
Repair Techniques	Involves stitching tears, patching holes, and addressing scratches.	Use appropriate tools like stitching awls and leather patches.	Focus on structural fixes. Stitching, patching, or reinforcing weak areas.	Periodic cleaning, conditioning, and minor repairs.
Restoration Goals	Aims to bring the leather back to its original or improved state.	Address color fade, restore luster, and enhance overall appearance.	Revive faded colors, remove stains, and rejuvenate worn surfaces.	Maintain or enhance the leather's visual appeal.
Tools and Products	Basic tools like stitching awls, leather patches, and conditioners.	Stitching tools, leather dyes, and color-matching products.	Specialized restoration products, leather cleaners, and conditioners.	Mild cleaners, leather conditioners, and protectants.
Real-Life Example	Repairing a torn seam on a leather jacket.	Stitching the tear with a leather needle and thread.	Restoring faded color on an old leather bag.	Regularly cleaning and conditioning a leather sofa.
Preventive Measures	Handle leather items with care to avoid tears and scratches.	Use protective measures like covers and avoid direct sunlight.	Store leather items properly to prevent wear and tear.	Keep leather away from harsh elements and moisture.

2. Leather Cleaning and Care

Welcome to Chapter 2. In this chapter, we will be focusing on cleaning and maintaining leather. Our goal is to help you establish a routine for leather care, prevent common issues through regular cleaning, understand the diverse cleaning needs of various leather types, and provide practical tips and recommendations for safe and effective cleaning solutions.

Leather Types and Care

Pigmented Leather:
- Finish applied for protection and color.
- Hardwearing with good liquid repellency.
- Suitable for various uses, especially for motorbike leathers or car interiors.

Aniline Leather:
- Natural appearance with no pigment finish.
- Absorbs water more readily, developing a unique patina over time.
- Often used for luxury goods.

Nubuck:
- Soft, velvety 'nap' created by sanding the grain side.
- Breathable but absorbs water or liquids.

Suede:

- It comes from the reverse side or by splitting the top layer.
- It is coarser than nubuck and is commonly used for apparel, bags, and footwear.

Pigmented Leather

Aniline Leather

Nubuck Leather

Suede Leather

Care Tips for Leather Types :

Pigmented Leather:

- Use soft brushes to remove dirt.
- Use various leather cleaners for maintenance.
- Colored shoe care products can even out scratches and abrasions.

Aniline Leather:

- Pre-treated with water-repellent care product.
- Clean with care using a dry brush or slightly damp cloth.
- Protect open-pore leather with waterproof products and non-absorbent leather with cream- or grease-based care items.

Nubuck and Suede:

- Protect with waterproofing sprays and avoid use in wet conditions.
- Remove dust and dirt with a medium-hard brush.
- Wash with specific leather-cleaning products and dry at room temperature.

Leather Furniture Care:

Pigmented Leather:

- Easy to clean; apply color repair products for scratches.

Aniline Leather:

- Handle with care, following manufacturer's recommendations.
- Test any product in a hidden area, which may darken the color.

Nubuck and Suede:

- Use a medium-hard brush for dust removal.
- Avoid staining; use protective sprays.
- Test protective spray or cleaning application in an inconspicuous area.

Cleaning and Maintaining Leather

Establishing a Routine for Leather Care:

Caring for leather is similar to taking care of something valuable. Just as we regularly maintain our homes and vehicles, establishing a consistent routine for leather care is crucial. For example, a straightforward weekly wipe-down with a damp cloth can prevent dust buildup, keeping your leather items in excellent condition.

Preventing Common Issues through Regular Cleaning:

Regular cleaning is not just about aesthetics; it's a proactive measure to prevent common issues like stains, discoloration, and deterioration. A leather bag neglected for months may develop permanent stains, whereas regular cleaning could have safeguarded its original charm.

Common Issues	Preventive Measures
Stains and Spills	Wipe spills immediately; avoid leaving items on leather surfaces.
Discoloration and Fading	Store leather items away from direct sunlight; use UV-protective sprays.
Deterioration and Cracking	Regularly condition leather with appropriate products.

Choosing the Right Cleaning Products

Understanding Leather Types and Their Cleaning Needs:

Leather is available in various types, each with unique characteristics such as full-grain, top-grain, aniline, etc. It is essential to understand these differences when choosing cleaning products. For example, full-grain leather may require a milder cleaner, while protected leather may tolerate a more robust solution.

Leather Type	Recommended Cleaning Products
Full-Grain	Mild leather cleaner; leather conditioner for conditioning.
Aniline	pH-neutral cleaner; aniline leather protector for added care.
Nubuck/Suede	Suede brush and cleaner; waterproofing spray for protection.

Recommendations for Safe and Effective Cleaning Solutions:

When selecting appropriate cleaning solutions for leather, it is crucial to consider the type of leather and the type of dirt or stain. You can use mild soap solutions or specialized leather cleaners to remove dirt and stains. However, it is crucial to always conduct a patch test in a hidden area before applying any product.

Cleaning Techniques for Different Leather Items/Products

Step-by-Step Guide for Cleaning Leather Furniture:

Cleaning leather furniture requires a gentle touch. For regular cleaning, use mild soap and water with a soft cloth or sponge.

To remove dust, vacuum with a soft brush attachment. Consider professional services for deeper cleaning.

Leather Furniture Type	Cleaning Techniques
Leather Sofas	Gently wipe with a damp cloth; avoid excess moisture.
Leather Chairs	Use a mild soap solution for regular cleaning; consult manufacturer guidelines.

Tips for Cleaning Leather Accessories and Clothing:

Specialized care is necessary for leather accessories and clothing. A leather handbag may benefit from a leather-specific cleaner, while a leather jacket might need occasional conditioning to retain suppleness.

Leather Item	Cleaning Tips
Leather Handbags	Use a mild leather cleaner; wipe gently with a soft cloth.
Leather Shoes	Clean with a damp cloth; use a shoe brush for polishing.

Leather Cleaning Guidelines

Preferred Cleaning Products:

- You can choose the leather cleaning products your Leather Supplier recommends for the best results.
- Select products formulated for compatibility with various leather types.

Avoid Using:

- High pH cleaners
- Cleaners with abrasives
- Cleaners containing alcohol or Butyl Cellosolve
- Strong solvents
- Saddle soap
- Mink oil
- Wax
- Furniture polish
- Glass cleaner
- Caustic household cleaners (e.g., soap or dish detergent)

Potential Risks:

- Certain cleaners vary in strength and compatibility with water-based leather finishes, potentially causing cracking or damage to the leather surface.

Heat and Sunlight Precautions:

- Avoid exposing leather to direct sources of heat.
- Prolonged exposure to heat sources and direct sunlight can harm leather; hence, it should be minimized.

Maintenance Tips:

- Regularly clean leather surfaces to prevent dirt buildup.
- Use a soft, damp cloth for routine cleaning.
- Dry leather naturally, avoiding artificial heat sources.

Stain Removal:

- Please take care of any stains on leather using approved cleaning methods, and avoid using excessive force as it can cause damage to the material.

Storage Recommendations:

- It's essential to store leather items in a cool, dry place with proper ventilation to prevent deterioration and mold/mildew growth.

Professional Assistance:

- Please seek professional advice before aggressively cleaning for stubborn stains or extensive damage.

Cleaners	Potential to Damage Water-Based Leather Finishes
High pH Cleaners	May negatively affect the water-based finish on leather.
Abrasive Cleaners	Can be too harsh and cause damage to the delicate leather finish.
Cleaners with Alcohol	May dry out the leather and compromise the finish over time.
Butyl Cellosolve-containing Cleaners	Can have adverse effects on water-based leather finishes.
Strong Solvents	Any cleaner with strong solvents has the potential to harm the finish.
Saddle Soap	Traditionally used for leather, but may not be suitable for water-based finishes.
Mink Oil and Wax-based Cleaners	Products containing mink oil or wax can alter the appearance and compromise integrity.
Furniture Polish	May contain substances detrimental to water-based leather finishes.
Glass Cleaner	Cleaners designed for glass may have components unsuitable for leather finishes.
Caustic Household Cleaners	Strong household cleaners can vary in compatibility and may harm water-based finishes.

Best Practices for Leather Cleaning and Maintenance

Approved Care Products:

- Utilize leather care products endorsed by your leather supplier or recognized brands in the industry.
- Include products like Finished Leather Cleaner, Cleaning Wipes, Conditioner, Protector, Ink and stain Remover Stick, Cotton Terry Cloth Rags, and a solution of distilled water with mild non-detergent soap.

Foundational Cleaning Steps:

- Initiate the process with meticulous vacuuming, employing a suction-style vacuum to eliminate debris and loose soil.
- Avoid using rotating brush-style vacuums to prevent potential damage to the leather.
- Focus on seams and crevices, common areas for particle accumulation.

Surface Cleaning Technique:

- Use a soft, clean rag dampened with an approved leather cleaner for routine cleaning.
- Apply the solution indirectly to the leather surface, avoiding direct application.
- Exercise caution to prevent damage, employing a pressure level similar to a firm handshake.

Cleaning Procedure:

- Apply the cleaner using moderate pressure in a circular motion with a cotton rag.
- Allow the leather to air dry naturally, refraining from applying additional heat.
- Repeat the process for heavily soiled areas, adjusting the rag as necessary.

Convenient Cleaning Wipes:

- Opt for Finished Leather Cleaning Wipes, available in practical resealable pouches, for a hassle-free cleaning option.

Avoid Over Application:

- Please don't forget to use the cleaning agent to avoid a tacky feel and potential transfer to clothing.
- If excess cleaner is applied, remove it with a dry cotton rag.

Stain and Spill Considerations:

- The outlined basic cleaning techniques are primarily for typical soil and may not address spills and stains effectively.
- Consider seeking professional advice or using specialized stain removal methods for specific stains.

Things to avoid in leather care and cleaning of old leather items

Avoid	Description
Harsh Chemicals	Chemicals such as bleach, ammonia, or household cleaners can strip away natural oils and damage the leather surface.
Excessive Water	Overexposure to water can cause leather to warp, crack, or develop water stains. Use sparingly and promptly dry leather items.
Direct Sunlight	Prolonged exposure to sunlight can cause leather to fade, dry out, and become brittle. Store leather items away from direct sunlight.
Heat Sources	Avoid placing leather items near heat sources such as radiators or fireplaces, as heat can cause leather to dry out and crack.
Abrasive Materials	Rough materials or abrasive brushes can scratch or scuff the leather surface, causing permanent damage. Use soft cloths or brushes designed for leather cleaning.
Oil-based Conditioners or Moisturizers	While conditioning is important, using oil-based products can darken leather or leave a greasy residue. Choose water-based or leather-specific conditioners.
Over-conditioning	Applying conditioner too frequently can saturate the leather and weaken its structure over time. Follow manufacturer recommendations for conditioning intervals.

Basics of Leather Repair

Welcome to Chapter 3 of "Leatherworking Revival." In this chapter, we will explore the fundamental principles of leather repair. You will learn how to understand the purpose of leather repair, identify when an item requires your attention, recognize different types of damage, and ensure you have all the necessary tools and materials before beginning any repair.

Clarifying the Purpose of Leather Repair:

Leather repair is more than just repairing visible damages. It is about preserving the functionality, aesthetic appeal, and longevity of your cherished leather items. Whether it is a tear in your leather jacket or a scratch on your favorite leather sofa, the aim of repair is to bring these items back to life by extending their use and enjoyment.

Recognizing When an Item Needs Repair:

Recognizing the right time to initiate a repair is crucial to prevent further damage. In some cases, signs of wear may be subtle, such as a weakening seam or a minor scratch. Identifying these early indicators helps you intervene before the damage becomes irreversible.

Signs of Damage	Action Needed
Loose Seams	Stitch or reinforce seams to prevent further unraveling.
Small Tears	Patch tears promptly to avoid enlargement.
Surface Scratches	Address scratches to prevent deeper damage.

Identifying Types of Damage

Understanding Tears, Scratches, and Stains:

Different types of damage require different approaches. Tears need stitching or patching, scratches may require color restoration, and stains may need specialized cleaning or restoration techniques.

Type of Damage	Recommended Actions
Tears	Stitching or patching, depending on tear size.
Scratches	Buffing, color restoration, or leather conditioning.
Stains	Cleaning with appropriate solutions; restoration for deep stains.

How Different Damages Require Different Approaches:

It is essential to understand that no universal leather repair solution exists. How you repair a tear is quite different from how you restore the color or remove a stubborn stain. By customizing your approach to the specific type of damage, you can ensure that the repairs are effective and long-lasting.

Essential Preparations Before Repairing

Gathering Tools and Materials:

The right tools and materials are crucial to ensure a successful repair process. In case of a tear, it is crucial to have a leather needle and strong thread, while appropriate coloring agents and conditioning products are needed for scratches. Gathering these essentials beforehand will help make the repair process smooth and hassle-free.

Type of Repair	Essential Tools and Materials
Stitching a Tear	Leather needle, strong thread, leather adhesive.
Restoring Color	Leather dye, applicator, leather conditioner.
Patching Holes	Leather patches, adhesive, stitching tools.

Table: Essential Tools and Materials for Common Repairs

Setting Up a Workstation for Successful Repair:

To facilitate repairs, it is essential to create a dedicated workspace that is well-lit and organized. This ensures safety, streamlines the process, and promotes accuracy in your repair efforts.

Workstation Component	Purpose
Adequate Lighting	Ensure clear visibility of the damaged area.
Organized Tools	Quick access to tools for an efficient repair process.
Protective Gear	Gloves and safety glasses for personal safety.

This chapter teaches you how to repair leather and provides you with the necessary knowledge and tools to give your old leather items a new lease of life.

Cuts, Rips And Tears - Repairing Process

To fix a damaged area:

- Start by cleaning it with rubbing alcohol and a cotton swab or pad.
- Cut out a piece of backing fabric with rounded edges larger than the damaged area.
- Insert the backing fabric into the damaged area using a spatula.

Next, choose the right color for your project by either using the primary colors or mixing and matching with the help of the color-matching guide included in the kit. Apply the compound to the damaged area with the spatula, paying attention to the edges and leveling the surface.

Allow the compound to dry for several hours. If needed, add additional layers to the damaged area. Once the compound is dry, use a cotton pad or swab with rubbing alcohol to buff the edges.

Burns And Holes- Repairing Process

- To prepare the damaged area, trim any jagged bits or burn marks with scissors or a knife. Then, clean the area using a cotton swab or pad with rubbing alcohol.

- Next, cut out a piece of backing fabric with rounded edges larger than the hole you must fix. Use a spatula to insert the fabric into the hole.

- You can use the primary colors provided in the kit or mix and match colors using the included color-matching guide to find the right color for your project.

- Fill the compound under and along the hole's edges, working your way from the outside to the center. Be sure to level the surface.

- Allow the compound to dry for several hours. If needed, apply additional layers.
- Once the compound is dry, buff the edges using a cotton pad or swab with rubbing alcohol.

Cuts, Rips And Tears

Burn Hole

Scratches And Peeling- Repairing Process

Prepare the Area:

Trim any peeling edges using scissors or a knife. Clean the damaged area with a cotton swab or pad soaked in rubbing alcohol.

Color Matching:

- Choose the perfect color for your project by mixing and matching from a color guide of main options.

Apply Compound:

- Applying a thin compound layer to the damaged area is recommended to ensure seamless coverage during repair.

Drying Process:

- Allow the compound to dry for several hours and reapply additional layers if necessary.

Buff the Edges:

- After the compound is dry, gently buff the edges with a cotton pad or swab soaked in rubbing alcohol to ensure a smooth and blended finish for a professional look.

Scratch

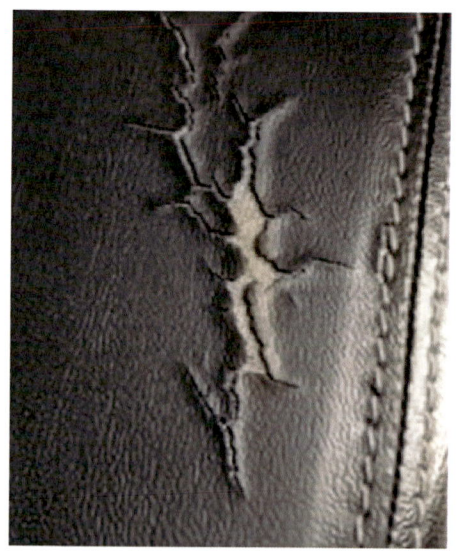

Peeling

Matching Color Process

- To prepare the color mixture, be aware that the color may dry slightly darker. Therefore, it's recommended to test the color mix on a small area before applying it to the larger surface.

- After applying the mixture, allow several hours to dry before confirming that the color is a good match. Also, ensure the compound and mixing jars are closed to avoid drying while waiting.

- When applying the compound, it's best to do it in layers. Before adding additional layers, ensure the color matches and allow several hours to dry between each layer.

- Remember, patience is vital. It might take a few attempts to match the perfect color, but achieving the desired result is worth it.

Matching Color

Leather and Vinyl Furniture Care Tips:

Regular Dry Cleaning:
- Use a dry microfiber cloth for regular dust removal.
- Avoid abrasive cloths; opt for gentle cleaning tools.
- Use a damp cloth with distilled water to wipe off dirt if needed.

Deeper Cleaning with Vacuum:
- Utilize a vacuum cleaner with a soft hose attachment and a soft-bristled brush.
- Clean the entire surface, including under cushions.
- Pay special attention to vacuuming crevices if cushions are non-removable.

Prompt Spill Management:
- Immediately blot away spills using a dry cloth or sponge.
- Minimize water usage; clean affected areas with as little water as necessary.
- Wipe the area dry promptly to prevent water-induced stains.

Mindful Placement:
- Avoid placing furniture near air vents, heaters, fireplaces, or in direct sunlight.
- Exposure to extreme conditions can lead to leather drying, cracks, or discoloration.
- Adhering to these care practices will help preserve the appearance and longevity of your leather or vinyl furniture.

Leather Furniture

4. Basics of Leather Restoration

Welcome to Chapter 4 of "Leatherworking Revival." In this chapter, we will explore the basics of leather restoration, including its concept, transformative nature, and how to assess color fade and loss of luster. We will guide you through reviving worn-out leather items and help you master the art of leather restoration. Let's get started!

Demystifying Leather Restoration

Clarifying the Concept of Leather Restoration:

Leather restoration is more than just fixing obvious damages; it is a skilled rejuvenation process. It involves returning the original beauty and vitality of leather that might have aged, faded, or lost its shine. Picture a classic leather chair that has endured decades of use- restoration can bring it back to life, preserving its charm for many years.

Example: Restoring a Faded Leather Bag

Consider a once-vibrant leather bag that has faded over time. Leather restoration would involve:

- *Assessing the extent of color loss.*
- *Selecting appropriate restoration products.*
- *Systematically restoring the bag's color to its former glory.*

Appreciating the Transformative Nature of Restoration:

Restoration is not just about fixing things; it's about rejuvenating the essence of your leather products. It's important to realize that restoration is not solely about repairing damages.

Instead, it's a process that enhances the appearance and uniqueness of your leather items, turning them into timeless treasures with renewed characteristics.

Example: Comprehensive Restoration of a Vintage Leather Chair

Imagine a vintage leather chair showing signs of wear, from faded color to minor scratches. Comprehensive restoration involves addressing each aspect—color restoration, scratch repair, and surface conditioning—to bring the chair back to its original splendor.

Assessing Color Fade and Loss of Luster

Understanding the Aesthetic Aspect of Restoration:

Aesthetic restoration focuses on the visual appeal of leather items. This involves restoring faded colors and rejuvenating the overall appearance, enhancing the richness of the leather, and bringing out its natural luster.

Example: Enhancing Luster in an Aged Leather Jacket
Restoration of an aged leather jacket involves reviving its color and luster through enhancing products, resulting in a renewed and polished appearance.

Steps for Evaluating and Planning Color Restoration:

It is crucial to evaluate the extent of color fade before diving into the process of color restoration. To do this, one must understand the original color, select the appropriate restoration products, and execute a step-by-step plan to achieve optimal results.

This chapter provides you with the necessary knowledge to begin your journey in leather restoration. By learning how to evaluate color fading and appreciate the transformative nature of restoration, you will uncover the art of reviving your leather items.

Steps	Description
Color Evaluation	Assess the current color state of the leather item.
Product Selection	Choose appropriate leather dyes or color-restoration products.
Test Application	Conduct a small test in an inconspicuous area to ensure compatibility.
Gradual Restoration	Apply color gradually, allowing for layering and achieving desired results.

Comprehensive Tips to Leather Restoration:

Introduction:

Leather is an adaptable material that requires appropriate maintenance to resist wear and tear, fading, and cracking. Follow these steps to restore leather effectively.

Understanding Leather Deterioration:

- Leather, being animal skin, can crack when it dries out.
- Environmental factors like dust, sunlight, oils, and moisture contribute to wear and tear.

Importance of Leather Restoration:

- Restoring leather involves reversing the drying process.
- Regular cleaning and Conditioning enhance leather longevity.

Six Steps for Leather Restoration:

- **Regular Cleaning**: Clean leather monthly to remove dirt, dust, and oil buildup. Use a gentle leather cleaning product for effective restoration.

- **Removing Scratches**: When dealing with scratches on leather, use a moisturizing conditioner to camouflage and repair them. However, it is essential to test the conditioner discreetly before applying it to the entire piece.

- **Restoring Cracked Leather**: Regularly hydrating leather with a conditioner can prevent cracks. Minor cracks can be resolved with conditioner, while professional assistance may be needed for deep cracks.

- **Conditioning**: Using a lint-free cloth, apply a non-toxic leather conditioner in thin coats. Allow absorption for at least two hours before wiping off excess.

- **Restoring Faded Leather**: Leather Honey Leather Conditioner can restore the original color of your leather. Apply it to the entire piece. For additional color adjustments, you can use leather color balm or dye.

- **Addressing Water Damage**: Use a dry cloth to wipe soaked leather, avoid heat, and restore moisture with Leather Honey Leather Conditioner.

Common Questions About Leather Restoration:

- Can damaged leather be restored?
- Yes, proper cleaning and Conditioning can restore most damaged leather.

- **Is leather restoration worth it?**

- Yes, considering the expense of genuine leather products, restoration extends their lifespan.

- **Can genuine leather be restored?**

- Yes, regular cleaning and Conditioning can make genuine leather look new.

- **How do you rehydrate rugged leather?**

- Use a premade conditioner, such as Leather Honey Leather Conditioner, to rehydrate rugged leather.

- **How do you rehydrate hard leather?**

For rehydrating hard leather, it's recommended to use a high-quality leather conditioner such as Leather Honey. Applying thin coats of conditioner and allowing it to absorb helps to restore lost moisture and make the leather supple again.

- **Can you restore cracked leather yourself?**

Regularly conditioning leather is crucial to prevent cracks. Use quality leather conditioner for minor cracks and seek professional assistance for deeper cracks.

- **What if the leather has water damage? Can it be fixed?**

Water-damaged leather can be restored by wiping away excess water with a dry cloth, avoiding heat, and allowing the leather to air dry. Following up with a reputable leather conditioner can help restore lost moisture and prevent further damage.

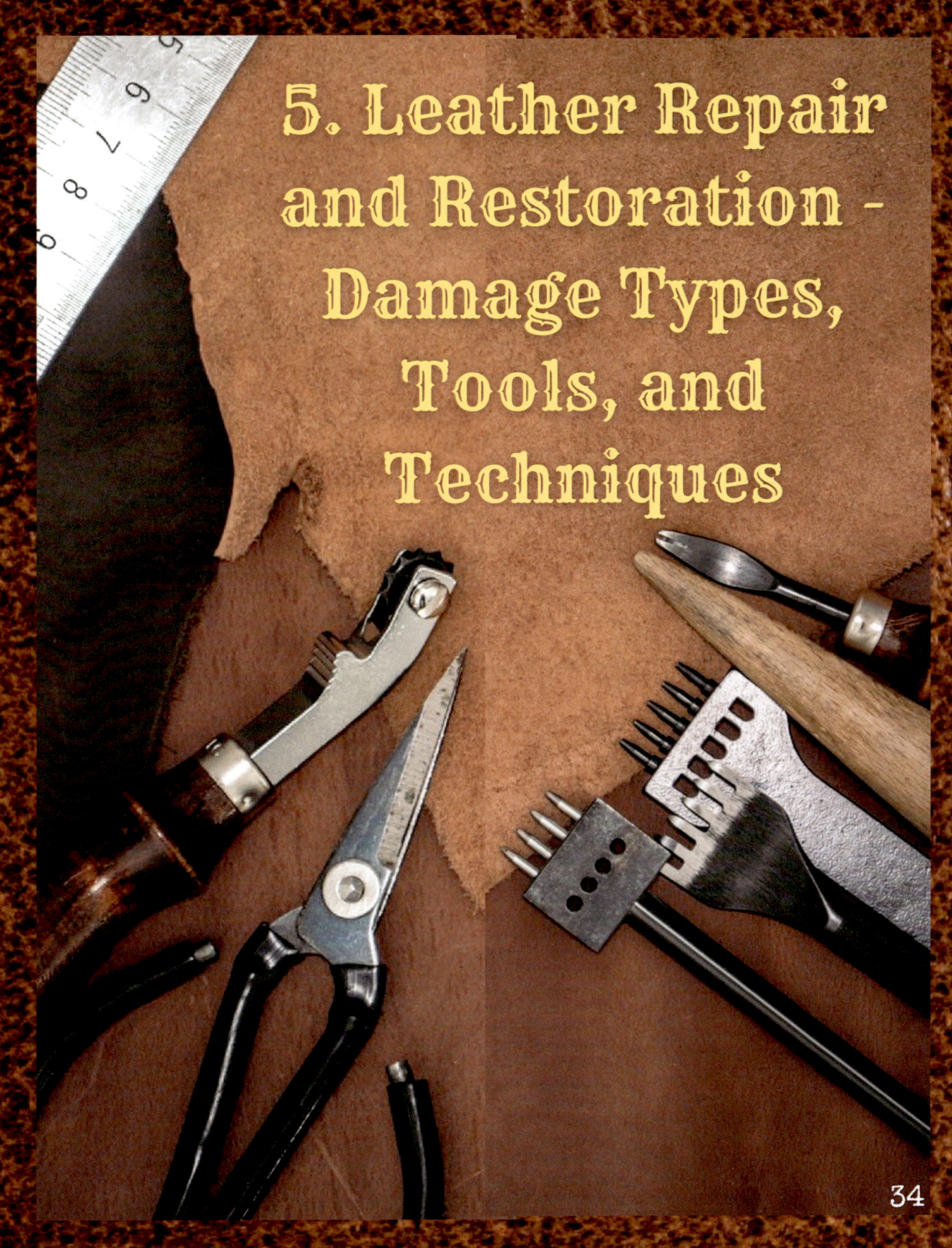

5. Leather Repair and Restoration - Damage Types, Tools, and Techniques

This chapter will explore the art of leather repair and restoration in detail. We will discuss the various types of damage that can affect our leather items and learn about the tools and techniques that can help us restore their former glory. By the end of this chapter, you will understand how to repair and rejuvenate your beloved leather

Purpose and Significance of Leather Repair and Restoration

Leather is a material that stands the test of time, but it is not immune to the effects of aging. The purpose of leather repair and restoration is not just about functionality but also about preserving the stories behind each piece and appreciating the skill and craftsmanship that went into creating it.

Connecting Repair and Restoration to the Overall Craft of Leatherworking

When we consider repair and restoration as essential components of leatherworking, it raises the craft to a higher level. It changes the process of fixing a tear or bringing back the color of the leather into an artistic pursuit, where every stitch and application is like a brushstroke on the canvas of your leather masterpiece.

Understanding Leather Damage

Types of Common Leather Damage

Tears and Rips	Scratches and Scuffs	Stains and Discoloration
From small nicks to significant tears.	Surface damage that mars the appearance.	Challenges that demand specialized techniques.
Importance of Timely Intervention		
Maintaining Structural Integrity: Timely repairs prevent tears, loose seams, or weakened areas, preserving the overall strength of the leather item.	**Avoiding Permanent Damage:** Addressing damage promptly prevents it from becoming permanent or significantly harder to restore over time.	**Preventing Costly Restoration/New Purchase:** Timely intervention prevents minor issues from escalating, avoiding the need for complex and costly restoration later.

Leather Repair and Restoration Tools

Cleaning Tools: Maintaining a Clean Canvas

Tool	When to Use	How to Use
Soft, Lint-Free Cloth	Before any restoration process to remove dust and dirt	Gently rub the surface of the leather in circular motions to lift dirt.
Bucket or Small Basin	Preparing cleaning solutions and rinsing off agents	Mix dishwashing soap and warm water for a cleaning solution. Rinse leather.
Dishwashing Soap	General surface cleaning before restoration	Mix in a bucket with warm water (1 part soap to 8 parts water).
Rubbing Alcohol	Removing deep stains on pigmented leather	Dilute and rub with a lint-free cloth, ensuring no staining on a patch test.

Leather Conditioning Tools: Nourishing and Enhancing Suppleness

Tool	When to Use	How to Use
Saddle Soap	During cleaning for conditioning leather	Apply a small dab on a wet cloth and wipe leather with circular motions.
Leather Conditioner	After cleaning to maintain moisture	Apply evenly with a soft cloth or applicator, allowing absorption into the leather.

Repair and Restoration Tools: Addressing Damage

Tool	When to Use	How to Use
Leather Repair Kit	Tackling cracks and splits in leather	Follow kit instructions; typically involves cleaning, applying filler, colorant, and treatment.
Glue	Fixing tears in leather	Apply with a needle, palette knife, or plastic knife, ensuring a secure bond.
Subpatches	Reinforcing tears in leather	Cut a patch larger than the tear, round corners, and use tweezers to insert under the tear.
Leather Binder (Liquid)	Binding fibers during repair process	Spread a thin layer with a sponge; repeat 3-5 times, removing excess around seams.

Coloring Tools: Restoring Aesthetic Appeal

Tool	When to Use	How to Use
Water-Based Leather Colorant	Restoring color, focusing on creases and cracks	Apply with a sponge or foam applicator, concentrating on hard-to-reach areas.
Spray Gun or Airbrush	Controlled application of colorant to prevent oversaturation	Fill the tool, spray fine coats, allow drying between applications, repeat as needed.
Colorant Shaker	Ensuring thorough mixing of colorant before application	Shake well to ensure colorant is adequately mixed, preventing uneven application.

Polishing and Finishing Tools: Achieving a Polished Look

Tool	When to Use	How to Use
Colorless Shoe Polish	Buffing scratched areas after vinegar treatment	Gently buff the area with a soft cloth after the vinegar treatment for a polished look.
Blow Dryer	Bringing dyes back to the surface on scratched leather	Turn to a medium setting, gently rub the scratched area, bringing dyes to the surface.
Weather-Resistant Protection Spray	Guarding against water damage	Apply every three months, keeping leather away from water and allowing delicate drying.

Repairing Cuts in Leather Furniture: Precision Tools

Tool	When to Use	How to Use
Tweezers	Precise insertion of subpatches under tears	Use tweezers to carefully insert subpatches under the tear, avoiding further damage.
Craft Glue	Ensuring a secure bond for tear repair	Apply to the underside of leather and subpatch, gluing the tear shut securely.
Leather Filler	Repairing small tears; can be force-dried	Apply in thin layers, force-dry if needed, repeat until the surface is level.
500 Grit Wet/Dry Sandpaper	Polishing rough spots on the repaired surface	Gently polish any rough areas with wet or dry sandpaper for a smooth finish.

Remember to carefully follow instructions for each tool and product and conduct patch tests as needed to ensure compatibility with the leather.

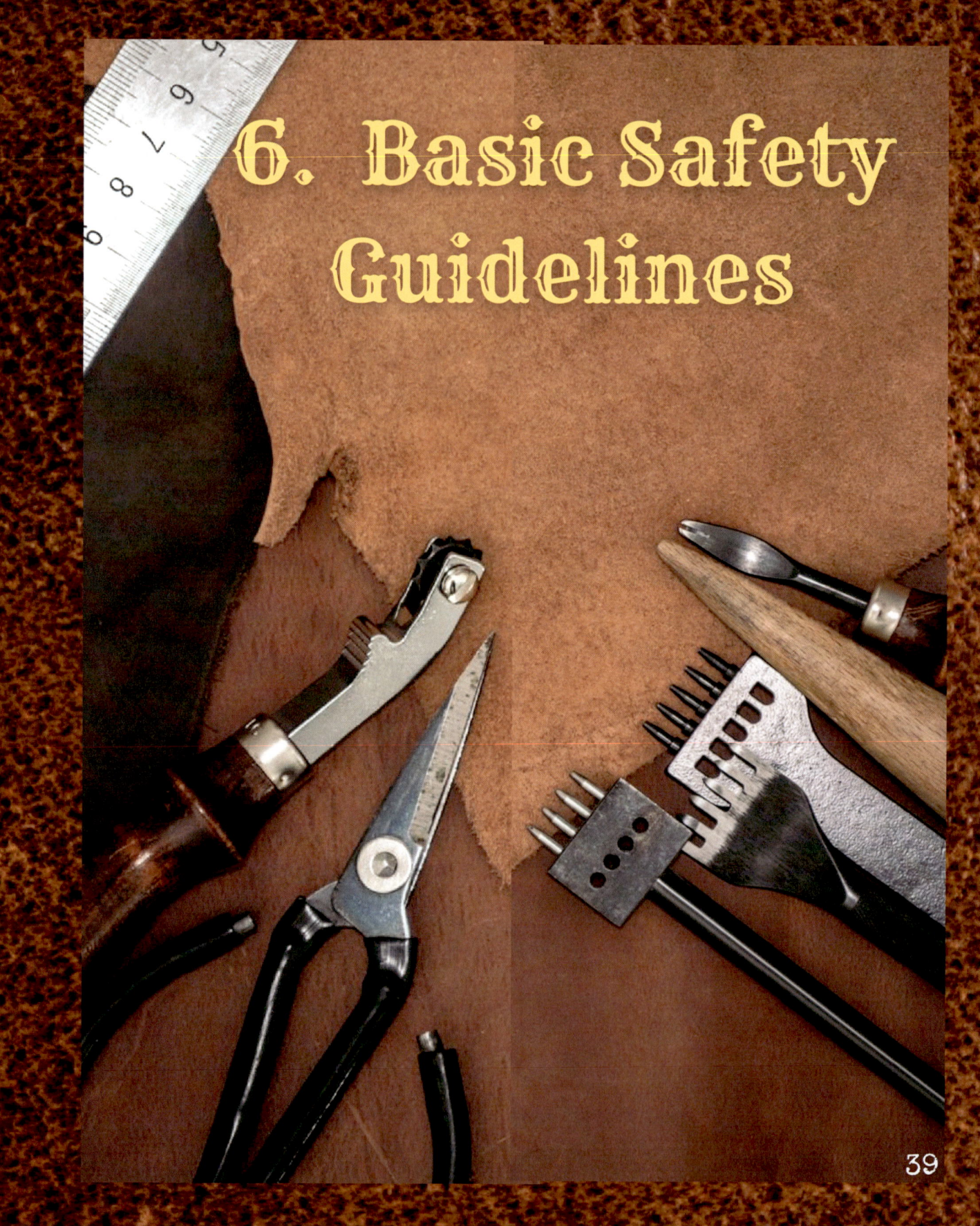

6. Basic Safety Guidelines

Safety and First Aid in Leatherworking

Many tools are used in leatherworking to safeguard against sharp edges and any untowardly incident.

The tools can be categorized into three categories as per their use:

- Tools that are pressed, like edgers, gouges, skivers, as well as some knives

 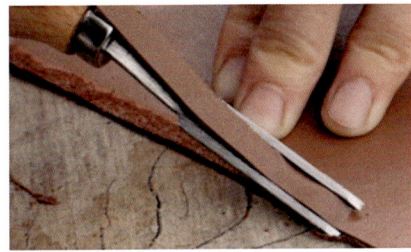

Skiver   Adjustable V-Gouge   edger

- Tools that are pulled, like swivel knives, utility knives, groovers, as well as strap cutters

 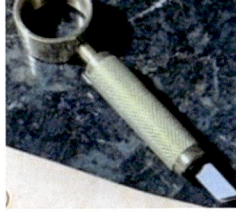 

Groover   Swivel Knife   Utility Knife

- Tools that are struck like punch and chisels

 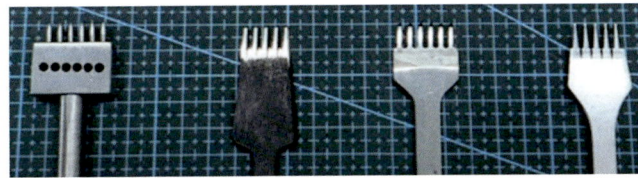

40

Tips :

- See that your tools are sharp-- a worn-out cutting tool is dangerous.

- Grip them firmly to guarantee complete control.

- Never place any part of your body on a cutting-edge path.

- Many dyes, cement, and coatings utilized in leatherworking include dangerous chemicals.

- To securely make use of these products, operate in a well-ventilated location.

- Thoroughly review and also adhere to all tag directions as well as cautions.

- Never ingest these chemicals or enable them to contact the skin.

- Shield your hands by putting on rubber gloves. Replace caps and also lids to prevent spills.

- Never make use of chemicals near an open fire. Instead, have a medical professional or emergency medical service phone number convenient in an emergency.

Cuts & Scratches

Cuts and scratches are wounds or openings in the skin and tissues that can permit germs to go into the body and cause infection.

Puncture wounds can be hazardous because they allow germs right into an injury that is tough to clean.

Remember, any individual enduring a major wound must be treated for shock and also seen by a physician immediately.

Steps of treatment :

For minor scratches and cuts:

- Clean the injury with soap as well as water.
- Apply disinfectant to help prevent infection.
- Keep the injury clean by covering it with an adhesive bandage.

For larger cuts:

- Apply direct stress to control bleeding.
- clean the injury to avoid infection.
- Cover the open wound with a sterile gauze pad or clean towel folded right into a pad.

For puncture wounds:

- Let the wound bleed so that any particle which went inside comes out.
- Wash the place with soap and water, use a sterilized bandage, and see a physician.

Skin Inflammation

Some dyes, cement, and finishes may trigger redness, a burning experience, itching, or swelling if they enter contact with the skin.

How to treat:

- Clean the affected area with soap and also water.
- Seek medical focus quickly if the irritation continues

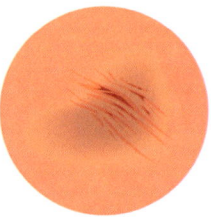

Consumed Poisoning

Poisoning is the most common reason for accidental fatality among young children. They will eat virtually anything, including the chemicals used in leatherworking, so keep such materials out of their reach.

Signs of poisoning include nausea or vomiting, stomach pains, burns around the mouth, and irregular breathing.

The most crucial indicator of poisoning is the presence of the toxin-- open bottles, spilled chemicals, or other proofs of what is being consumed by the kid.

How to treat:

- Right away, find a telephone, take any poisonous substance containers you see along with you, and call the poison control center of the neighborhood.
-Call the nearest doctor.
- Only offer something by mouth if you are told to do so by medical professionals.

Best Practices for Beginners

- Use protective gear like gloves, eye goggles, and masks when working with chemicals and devices.

- Maintain your work area clean and also organized to avoid mishaps.

- Use sharp blades and tools to stay safe from cuts or scratches after applying pressure.

- Always cut away from your body and ensure your fingers are out of the way.

- You can use a cutting mat to avoid damage to your work surface and keep your blades sharp.

- When using a swivel knife, constantly cut at a 45-degree angle and use a cutting board to avoid damage to your blade.

- When stamping or tooling leather, utilize a mallet instead of a hammer to stop harmful your tools.

- Use the proper dimension as well as the weight of the hammer for every device to stay clear of damage and boost accuracy.

- Use a leather punch to make clean and exact holes in your natural leather.

- Use a leather burnisher to smooth and polish the sides of your natural leather after cutting.

- Use natural leather adhesive moderately and adhere to the manufacturer's guidelines.

- Utilize a leather conditioner to keep your leather flexible and also avoid splitting.

- Use a natural leather color or end up in a well-ventilated location to prevent breathing in fumes.

- Prevent utilizing sharp objects like scissors or knives to pry open stitches or joints, as it can harm your leather.

- Practice good ergonomics to stay clear of repetitive strain injuries. Take breaks regularly and also extend your hands and also wrists regularly.

- Use caution when utilizing a hammer or mallet. Ensure your fingers are free from the striking area and prevent the hard-hitting of your devices.

- Ensure ventilation when dealing with chemicals such as dyes or adhesives. Use a respirator if required and stay clear of breathing in fumes or vapors.

7. Leather Resoration Projects

(1) Restoring Old Leather Boots

Step 1: Preparation

- You can cover your workspace with a newspaper or rag.
- Remove the laces to make cleaning easier.
- Insert shoe shaper or shoe trees to maintain the shape during restoration.

Step 2: Remove Dirt

- You can use a horsehair brush to brush off caked-on dirt and dust.
- Ensure thorough coverage, reaching all gaps and crevices.

Step 3: Saddle Soap

- Choose a leather-specific soap like saddle soap containing lanolin or beeswax.
- Test the product on an inconspicuous spot to check for color compatibility.
- Use an applicator brush to create a lather, applying it across the boots' surface, including the tongue.
- Wipe off excess soap with a towel and let the boots air dry for at least 15 minutes.

Horse Hair Shoe Brush

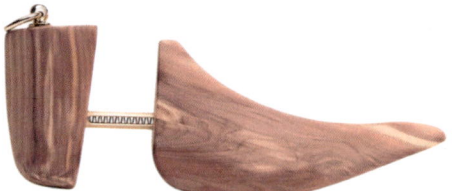

Shoe Shaper/Tree

Old Leather Boot

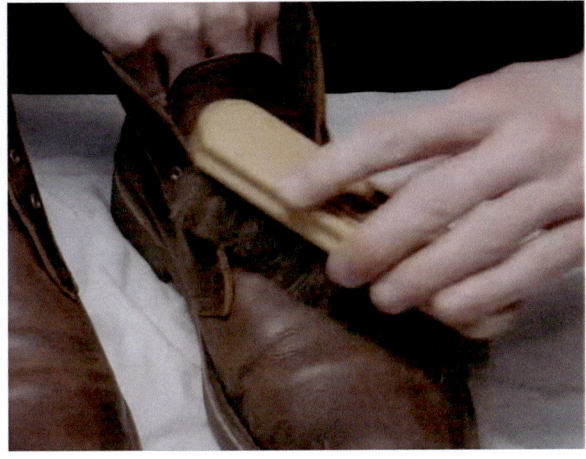

Remove Dirt   Apply Saddle Soap

Step 4: Removing Creases

- Ensure shoe trees are in place, making the shoes in shape.
- Warm up a clothing iron to the cotton setting.
- Place a damp towel on the front of the shoes to prevent heat damage.
- Gently iron over the boot, letting the heat, steam, and gentle pressure work out creases.
- Remove the cloth and stretch out the remaining lines lightly with your fingers.

Step 5: Conditioning

- Use a leather conditioner to replenish lost moisture.
- Apply the conditioner with a soft cleaning rag, filling gaps and crevices.
- Pay special attention to spots that flex and bend during walking.
- Wipe off excess conditioner and allow the boots to dry for one or two hours.

Step 6: Recoloring

- Choose a cream polish in a color closely matching your boots.
- Perform a spot test before applying it to all the boots.
- Use a small applicator brush to spread the cream around the boots' upper in small circles.
- Allow the cream to dry for five minutes, then use a clean horsehair brush to buff the leather.

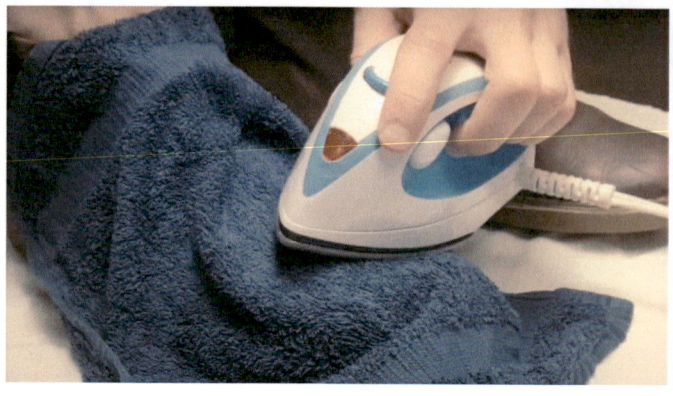
Removing Creases

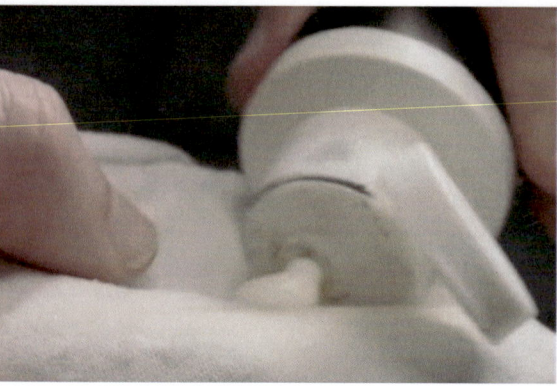
Put conditioner into a cloth

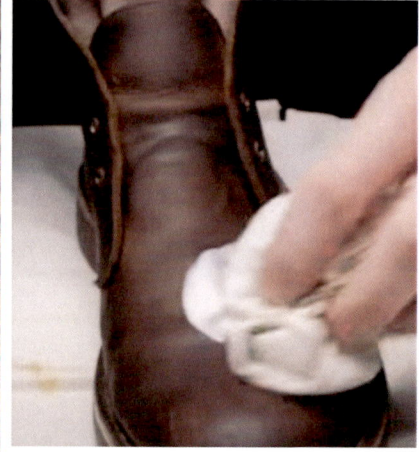
Applying Conditioner

Cream Polish

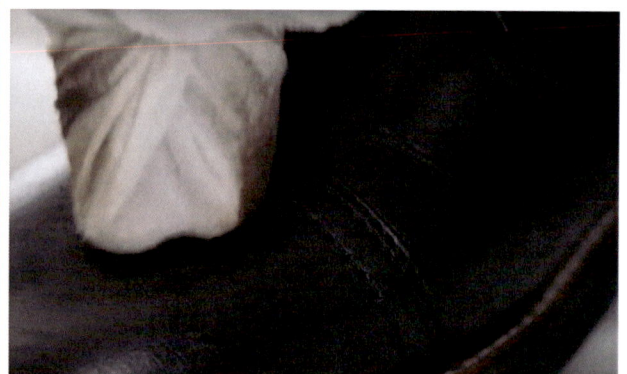
Applying Wax Polish

Restored Boot

- Avoid using the same brush used for dirt removal.
- For formal boots, apply a wax polish for additional shine and protection.
- Reinsert the laces, and you're done!

(2) Fix Rips and Cracks in Your Leather Sofa/Chair

Assessment: Examine the leather furniture, identifying areas with cracks, wear, and rips.

Cleaning: Clean the entire area to be treated, removing any dirt or contaminants. This ensures that the dye adheres appropriately.

Dye Application:

- Shake the leather dye bottle to ensure uniform color.
- Apply the dye to a sponge and spread it over the affected areas. Ensure the dye penetrates cracks and worn spots.
- Let the first coat dry, and repeat the process for additional coats until satisfied with the color depth.

Leather Filler Application:

- Assess the extent of cracking and wear. If more profound than the thickness of a fingernail, use a leather repair filler.
- Open the leather repair filler kit and apply it to the cracks, smoothing it into the damaged areas.
- Use a paper template to maintain the leather's natural curvature while applying filler for seamless repair.
- Allow the filler to dry, checking for smoothness. If necessary, lightly sand the repaired areas.

Drying: Use a hairdryer or allow the treated areas to air dry thoroughly before proceeding.

Dye Reapplication: Add additional leather dye to achieve the desired color and coverage. Dry between coats.

Sealing: Once the color and repair are satisfied, apply a leather sealer to protect and seal the dyed and filled areas.

- **Final Touches**: Ensure the repaired areas are smooth and match the surrounding leather. If necessary, use sandpaper to refine the finish.

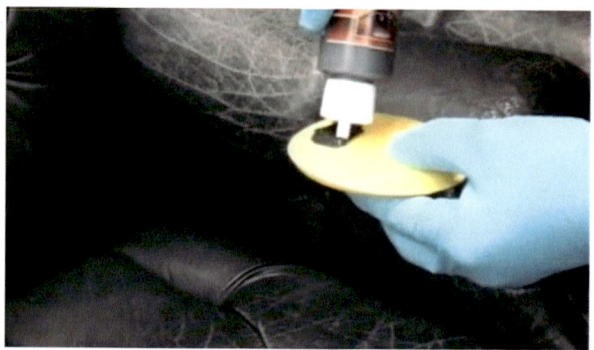
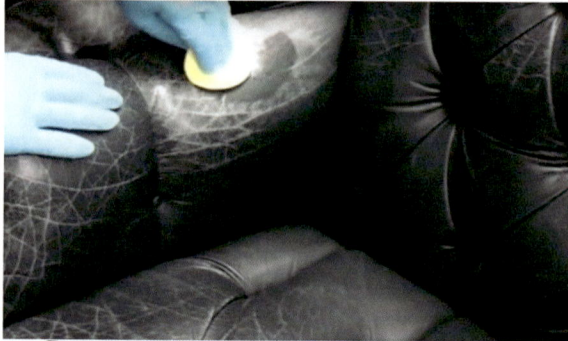

Applying Dye

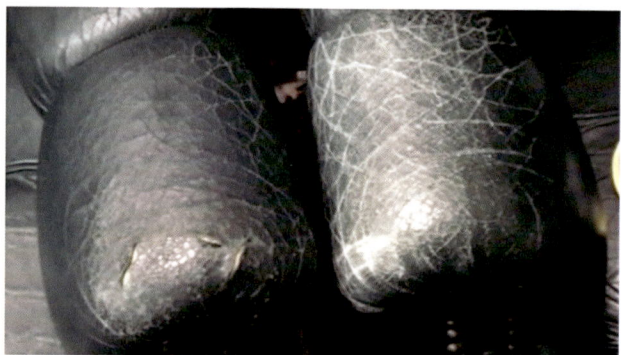

Cracks & Wear

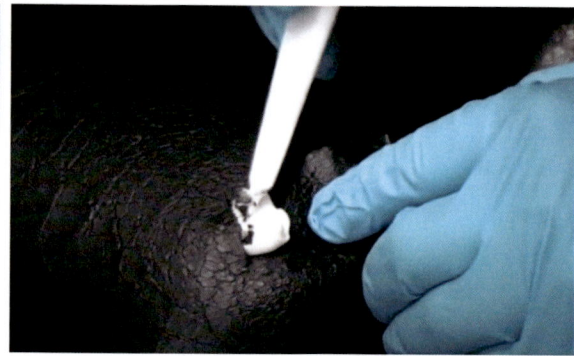

Applying Filler

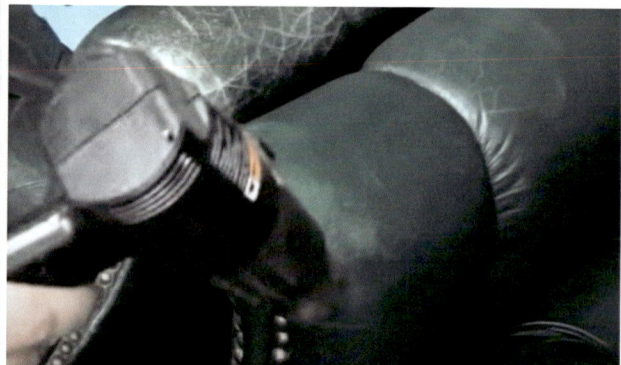

Dry it using Blower/Dryer

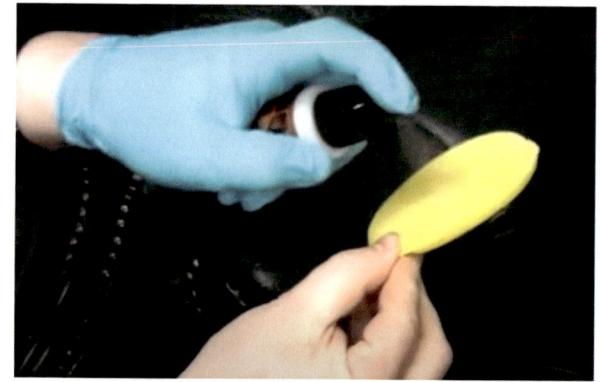

Apply Sealer

Reapply Dye and Dry it

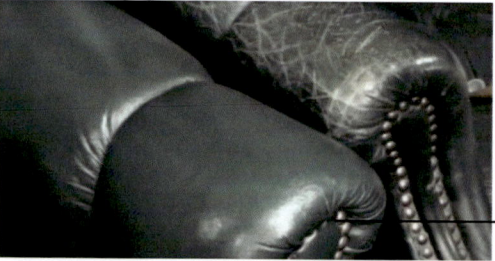

Restored Chair/Sofa

(3) Leather Bag Restoration

Materials Required :

- Saddle soap
- Neat's-foot oil or leather conditioner
- Clean cloths
- Horsehair brush (optional)
- Metal polish (optional)
- Sandpaper (120-grit or 240-grit)
- Gum tragacanth or burnishing tool (optional)
- Leather polish (optional)

Saddle Soap   Leather Conditioner   Clean Cloth

Horse Shoe Brush   Sand Paper   Gum tragacanth

Cleaning:

- **Apply saddle soap:** Use a damp cloth to apply a small amount of saddle soap, thoroughly wiping down the entire leather surface to remove dirt and grime.

- **Let it dry:** Allow the leather to air-dry completely for 10-20 minutes or longer.

- **Brush off excess:** Brush off any remaining saddle soap residue using a clean cloth or a horsehair brush for a polished look.

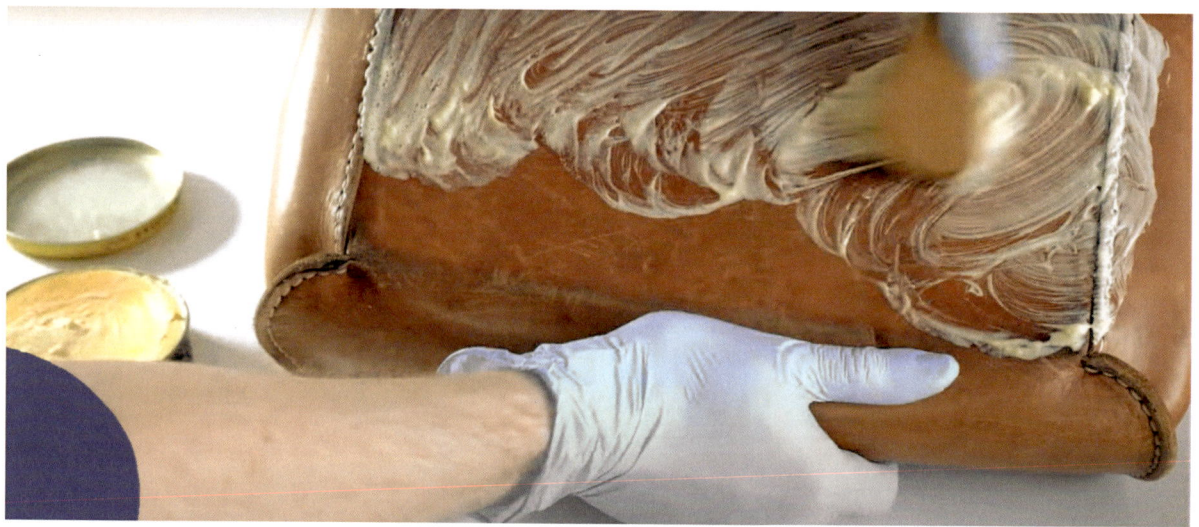
Applying Saddle Soap

Conditioning:

- **Apply conditioner:** Apply a thin, even coat of neat-foot oil or leather conditioner to replenish the leather's oils, enhancing suppleness and preventing cracking.

- **Let it absorb:** Allow the oil or conditioner to absorb completely, leaving it for several hours or overnight for optimal results.

- **Buff off excess:** Buff off any excess oil or conditioner with a clean cloth, leaving the leather with a natural sheen.

Optional Steps:

- **Clean metal hardware:** If the bag has metal hardware, use metal polish to remove dirt and tarnish. Be cautious not to get polish on the leather.

- **Burnish the edges:** If desired, burnish the edges using sandpaper (120-grit or 240-grit) and gum tragacanth or a burnishing tool to achieve a smooth, polished finish.

- **Apply leather polish:** For an additional layer of protection and shine, apply a thin coat of leather polish, ensuring an even application.

Final Touches:

- **Let it dry:** Allow the bag to dry completely before storing or using it to avoid any smudges.

Additional Tips:

- Test any cleaning or conditioning products on a small, inconspicuous area before applying them to the entire bag.

- Avoid using harsh chemicals or water, as these can damage the leather.

- Store the bag in a cool, dry place away from direct sunlight.

- Repeat the cleaning and conditioning process as needed, typically every few months or as the leather starts to feel dry.

(4) Leather Satchel Restoration

Step 1: Assessment and Preparation

- **Examine the satchel:** Assess the condition, noting areas that require attention, such as damaged straps or hardware.

- **Gather materials:** Assemble the necessary materials, including saddle soap, Neat's-foot oil or leather conditioner, clean cloths, horsehair brush, metal polish (optional), sandpaper (120-grit or 240-grit), gum tragacanth or burnishing tool (optional), leather polish (optional), and Maisy linen thread.

Step 2: Cleaning and Initial Restoration

Saddle soap application:
- Dampen a cloth and apply a small amount of saddle soap.
- Wipe down the entire leather surface to remove dirt and grime.

Drying:
- Allow the leather to air-dry completely for at least 10-20 minutes.

Brush off excess:
- Use a clean cloth or horsehair brush to remove any remaining saddle soap residue.

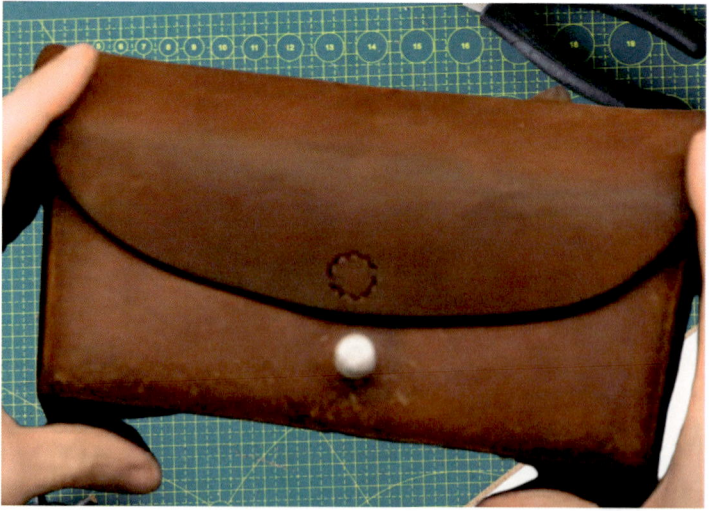

Old Leather Satchel

Step 3: Conditioning and Restoration

- Neat's-foot oil or conditioner application:
- Apply a thin coat of Neat 's-foot oil or leather conditioner to replenish the leather's oils.
- Allow absorption for several hours or overnight.

Buffing:
- Buff off any excess oil or conditioner with a clean cloth for a natural sheen.

Step 4: Optional Steps

Clean metal hardware (if applicable):
- Use metal polish to clean metal hardware, avoiding contact with the leather.

Burnishing the edges (if desired):
- Use sandpaper (120-grit or 240-grit), gum tragacanth, or a burnishing tool to achieve smooth, polished edges.

Applying leather polish (optional):
- For extra protection and shine, apply a thin coat of leather polish.

Step 5: Creating a Replacement Closing Strap

Identifying the sacrificial piece:
- Locate a redundant strap to create a replacement closing strap.

Tracing and cutting:
- Trace the new piece, considering the hidden portion underneath the flaps.
- Bevel the edges for a comfortable touch.

Making stitching holes:
- Mark and make stitching holes, following the slant given by the original Saddler.

Stitching:
- Use Maisy linen thread, prepped with beeswax, to stitch the new piece in place.

Step 6: Final Touches

Punching holes and cutting relief:
- Punch holes for attaching the closing strap and cut any necessary relief.

Adding D-rings (if desired):
- Attach D-rings to the back for additional functionality.

Applying final coat:
- Apply a final coat of Safir renovatoeur for shine and protection.

Restored Leather Satchel

(5) Faded Leather Jacket Restoration

Worn Leather Jacket

Step 1: Gather Necessary Supplies:

- Horsehair brush
- Two microfiber towels
- Distilled water
- Saddle soap or mild leather cleaner
- Leather conditioner/saddle butter

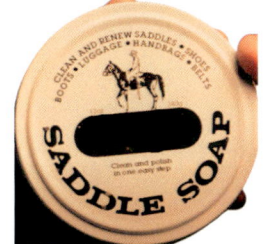

Preparation:

- Brush off dirt and dust from the jacket using the horsehair brush.

Brush off the dirt

Wipe off with Towel

Apply Saddle Soap

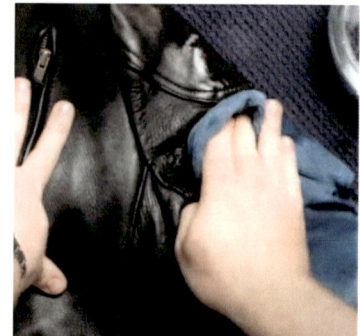

Buffing

Initial Cleaning:

- Dampen one microfiber towel with distilled water.
- Wipe down the entire jacket to remove remaining dirt or grime.

Saddle Soap Application:

- Place a towel underneath the jacket to catch excess moisture.
- Dampen a brush and work up a lather with saddle soap.
- Apply the saddle soap in a fine coat over the entire jacket.

Buffing:

- Allow saddle soap to dry for 10-15 minutes.
- Use a damp rag to buff the leather and remove excess soap thoroughly.

Drying:

- Let the jacket dry for 30 minutes to an hour at room temperature.

 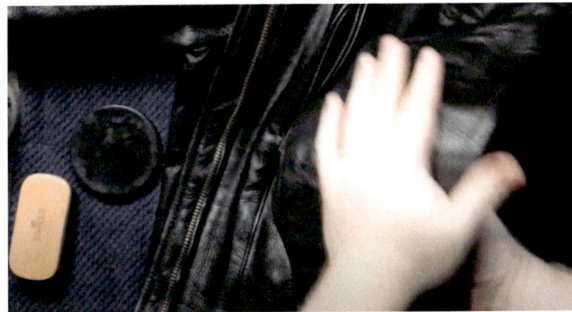

Apply Conditioner

Apply Waterproofing Paste

Conditioning:

- Warm a small amount of leather conditioner in your hands.
- Massage conditioner into the leather, focusing on dry or cracked areas.
- Leave the conditioner on overnight for optimal absorption.

Final Buffing:

- Use a dry microfiber towel to buff the leather and remove excess conditioner gently.

Maintenance:

- Between conditioning sessions, use a damp towel to wipe down the jacket.
- Apply a thin layer of Vaseline for added moisture and protection.

Optional Waterproofing:

- Consider applying waterproofing paste or silicone spray for additional protection.

Regular Care:

- Repeat the cleaning and conditioning process as needed, aiming for at least once a year.

Post-Restoration:

- Admire the restored appearance of the leather jacket and share your experience with others.

(6) Leather Pouch Restoration

Step 1: Assessment and Cleaning

- Begin by examining the leather pouch for any visible dirt, stains, or dryness.
- Use oak wood leather wipes designed for everyday furniture cleaning to wipe the pouch's surface gently.
- Ensure the pouch's exterior and interior are cleaned to remove accumulated dirt or residue.
- Consider using a leather-specific cleaning cloth to avoid drying out the leather further.
- Pay attention to the edges and corners, as they may require extra care during cleaning.
- Fold the cloth to access tight spaces within the pouch and remove any hidden dirt or grime.

Old Leather Pouch

Leather Wipes

Step 2: Conditioning with Leather Balsam

- Select a high-quality leather balsam product, such as Kiwi Dave's leather balsam, which is predominantly made of beeswax and natural plant-based ingredients.
- Take a clean microfiber cloth and apply a small amount of leather balsam.
- To test the results, begin rubbing the balsam onto the leather pouch, starting from the back or an inconspicuous area.
- Work the balsam into the leather in circular motions, ensuring even coverage across the entire surface.
- Monitor the absorption of the balsam into the leather, as dry leather may absorb the product quickly.
- Consider applying multiple coats of balsam for thorough conditioning, especially if the leather appears exceptionally dry.
- Allow the balsam to dry completely between each application to avoid any greasy residue.

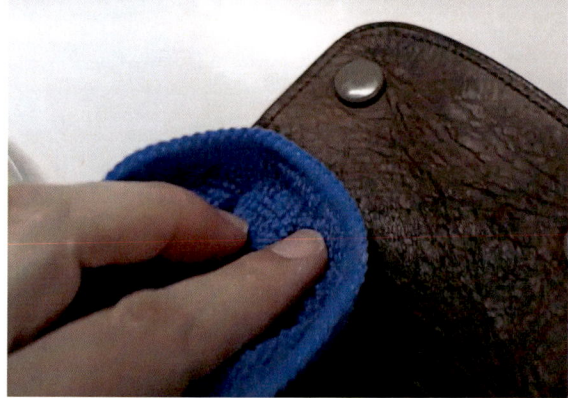

Applying Leather Balsam

Step 3: Final Inspection and Usage

- Once the leather pouch has absorbed the balsam and dried, inspect it for any remaining dryness or imperfections.
- Assess the overall appearance and texture of the leather to ensure it feels supple and revitalized.
- Note any wrinkles or creases that may be present, often characteristic of aged leather.

- Test the functionality of the pouch by inserting suitable items such as notebooks and pens to ensure proper fit.
- Securely close the pouch and admire the restored condition, appreciating its renewed usability.
- Optionally, consider periodic maintenance by applying additional layers of balsam over time to maintain the leather's quality.

Following these steps for restoring a leather pouch, you can effectively clean, condition, and revitalize aged leather, prolonging its lifespan and preserving its aesthetic appeal. Enjoy the satisfaction of breathing new life into vintage leather goods and continue to appreciate their timeless charm for years.

(7) Leather Belt Restoration

Step 1: Initial Assessment

- Begin by closely examining the leather belt to assess its current condition, noting any visible signs of wear, dryness, or discoloration.

Step 2: Gathering Materials

Gather the necessary materials for the restoration process, including:
- Sandpaper (150 grit and 220 grit)
- Vaseline petroleum jelly or a similar leather conditioning product

Worn out Leather Belt

Step 3: Preparation

- Optionally, mark a section of the belt with masking tape to compare the before and after results of the restoration process.

Step 4: Sanding

- Start the restoration process by using 150-grit sandpaper to sand the top layer of the belt gently.
- Be cautious not to sand too aggressively, as this may thin out the leather excessively.
- Once the desired amount of the top layer has been removed, switch to 220-grit sandpaper to smooth the surface further.

Step 5: Cleaning

- After sanding, wipe the belt with a clean cloth to remove debris or residue from the sanding process.
- Before proceeding to the next step, ensure the belt surface is clean and free from particles.

Sanding

Step 6: Conditioning

- Apply a generous amount of Vaseline petroleum jelly or a similar leather conditioning product onto the entire surface of the belt.
- Use a clean cloth or applicator to spread the conditioning product over the leather surface evenly.
- Note that the leather may initially darken in color due to the application of the conditioning product.

Step 7: Absorption and Finishing

- Allow the belt to sit for some time to allow the petroleum jelly to be absorbed into the leather.
- Optionally, spread out any excess conditioning product to ensure even absorption and prevent over-saturation.
- Remove any masking tape used for comparison to observe the difference in appearance between the treated and untreated sections.

Step 8: Final Inspection

- Once the conditioning product has been absorbed and the belt has dried, inspect the entire belt for uniformity and any remaining imperfections.
- Note any color, texture, and overall appearance improvements compared to the initial assessment.

Apply Vaseline for Conditioning

Step 9: Completion

- Complete the process by admiring the renewed appearance and functionality upon satisfactory restoration of the leather belt.
- Consider repeating the restoration process periodically to maintain the leather belt's condition and extend its lifespan.

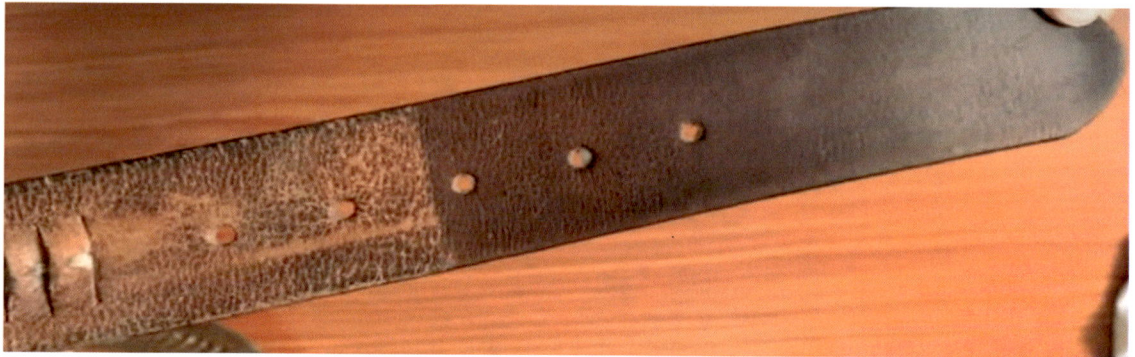

Completed Part of the Belt

(8) White Leather Shoe Restoration

Step 1: Assessment

- Begin by assessing the condition of the white leather shoes, noting any wrinkles, creases, scuffs, or discoloration that need attention.

Step 2: Preparation

- Remove the shoelaces from the shoes to facilitate thorough cleaning and restoration.

Step 3: Cleaning

- Rinse the shoes with soapy water and gently scrub them with a soft brush or cloth to remove surface dirt and grime.
- For stubborn stains or yellowing, soak the shoes overnight in a mixture of water and a small amount of bleach.

Step 4: Orbital Cleaning

- Utilize an orbital tool or a white magic eraser pad to clean the leather surface effectively.
- Apply soapy water to the cleaning tool and gently rub it over the leather in circular motions, exerting moderate pressure to lift stains and dirt.

Step 5: Heat Treatment for Creases

- Stuff the shoes with a moist rag to provide structure and fill any empty spaces.
- Apply a small amount of water to the creased areas of the leather.
- Using a heat gun or a clothes iron set to a low heat setting, carefully apply heat to the creased areas while avoiding prolonged exposure to prevent damage to the leather.
- Continue to apply heat evenly, moving the tool around to address all creases until the leather softens and reshapes.

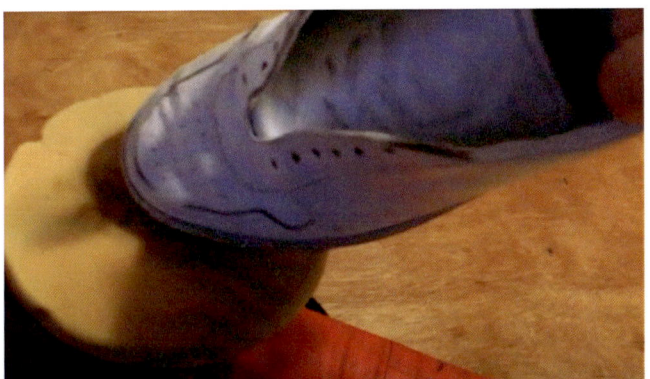
Orbital Cleaning

Heat Treatment/Ironing

Step 6: Optional Ironing Technique

- Alternatively, use a clothes iron set to a low heat setting and a damp cloth between the iron and the leather to iron out creases.
- Gently press the iron over the damp cloth-covered leather, moving it in a circular motion to smooth out wrinkles and creases.

Step 7: Final Touches

- After completing the heat treatment or ironing process, allow the shoes to cool and dry thoroughly.
- Inspect the shoes for any remaining scuffs or imperfections requiring touch-up with leather paint or conditioner.

Step 8: Re-lacing and Final Inspection

- Once the shoes are fully restored and dried, re-lace them with clean shoelaces.
- Conduct a final inspection to ensure the shoes are clean, smooth, and free from noticeable imperfections.

Step 9: Maintenance

- To maintain the restored condition of the white leather shoes, store them properly in a cool, dry place away from direct sunlight.
- Regularly clean and condition the leather to prevent future staining, yellowing, or creasing.

Restored White Leather Shoe

(9) Leather Briefcase Restoration

Step 1: Initial Assessment

- Begin by examining the leather briefcase for any visible damage, such as loose handles, fading, water spots, or cracking.

Step 2: Cleaning with Saddle Soap

- Use saddle soap and water to gently clean the surface of the briefcase, removing dirt, grime, and surface impurities.
- Apply saddle soap with a soft cloth or sponge, working it into a lather to clean the leather surface effectively.

Step 3: Nourishing the Leather

- Apply Saphir Creme Universal or a suitable leather conditioner to nourish and moisturize the leather, restoring suppleness and enhancing color.
- Use a liberal amount of conditioner, especially on dry or damaged areas, to ensure thorough coverage and rejuvenation of the leather.

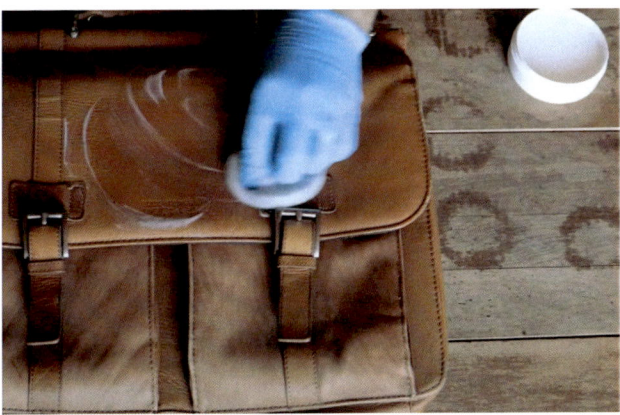

Apply Saddle Soap

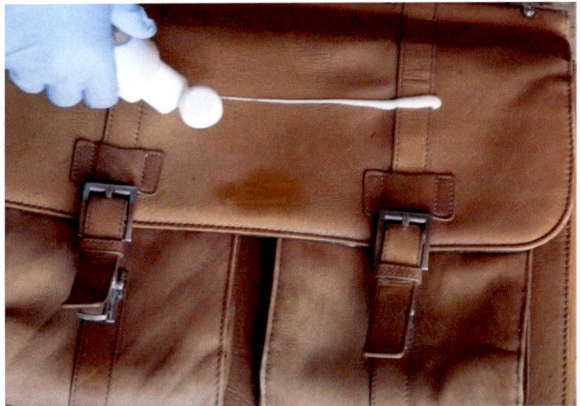

Apply Leather Conditioner

Step 4: Addressing Oil Spots and Stains

- Identify any oil spots or stubborn stains on the leather surface and take appropriate measures to address them.

- Use acetone or a suitable stain remover to treat oil spots and stains, following manufacturer instructions and testing on a small, inconspicuous area first.

Step 5: Dyeing the Leather (Optional)

- If desired, dye the leather using a suitable leather dye to enhance color or restore faded areas.
- Apply the dye evenly using a brush or sponge, ensuring thorough coverage and allowing adequate drying time between coats.

Step 6: Creating a Rustic Patina (Optional)

- Experiment with creating a rustic patina by intentionally distressing the leather with acetone or other techniques to achieve a weathered, vintage look.
- Apply acetone selectively to create areas of contrast and depth, mimicking the appearance of aged leather.

Step 7: Adding Burnishing and Final Touches

- Use a sponge or soft cloth to apply burnishing wax or shoe polish to the leather surface, enhancing shine and depth of color.
- Work the polish into the leather using circular motions, focusing on areas that require additional sheen or protection.

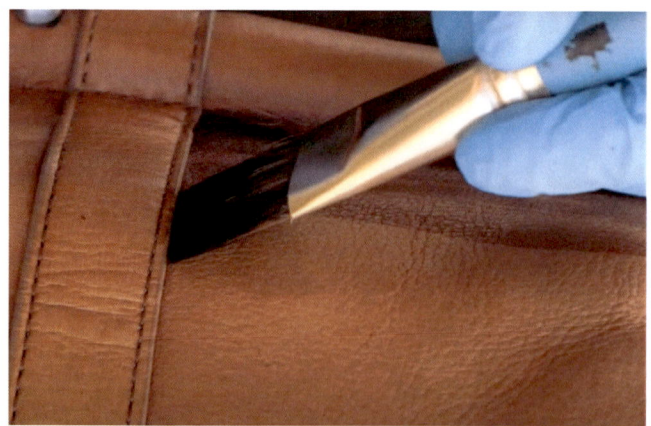

Apply Dye

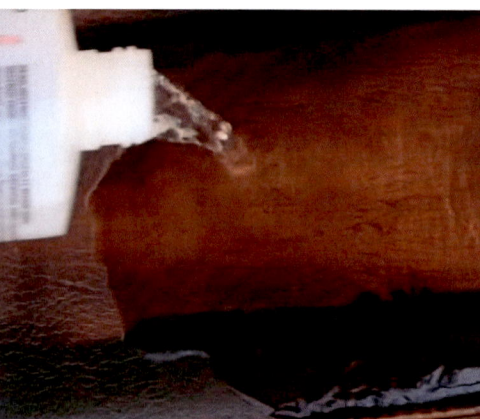

Pour Acetone

Apply Shoe Polish

Restored Briefcase

(10) Restoring a Leather-Wrapped Steering Wheel

Step 1: Cleaning the Steering Wheel

- Clean the leather-wrapped steering wheel with isopropyl alcohol, preferably 90% concentration, to remove dirt and grime from the surface.

Step 2: Repairing Small Tears and Dents

- Identify any small tears or dents on the steering wheel surface.
- Measure a small amount of super glue onto a piece of cardboard and apply it to the damaged areas using a needle or toothpick.
- Flatten the glue and remove excess, then press it firmly using a flattening tool. Remove any flappy bits and fill any gaps.

Step 3: Sanding the Repaired Areas

- Use 320-grit wet or dry sandpaper to sand the repaired areas toward the original tear. Sand back and forth until smooth, ensuring evenness across the surface.
- For deeper gouges, create an epoxy mixture using super glue and baking soda to fill the void. Apply the mixture and smooth it out to level the surface.

Clean with Isopropyl Alcohal

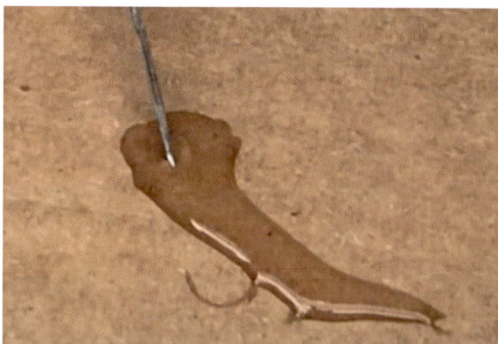 

Put Super Glue into wear and tear

Apply Sandpaper

Step 4: Polishing

- Polish the repaired areas using 500-grit sandpaper to achieve a smooth finish. Wipe off any dust or residue from the surface.

Step 5: Color Testing

- Prepare a custom color for the steering wheel if necessary. Apply the color to the repaired areas to match the original shade.
- Evaluate the color match and make adjustments as needed for a seamless blend.

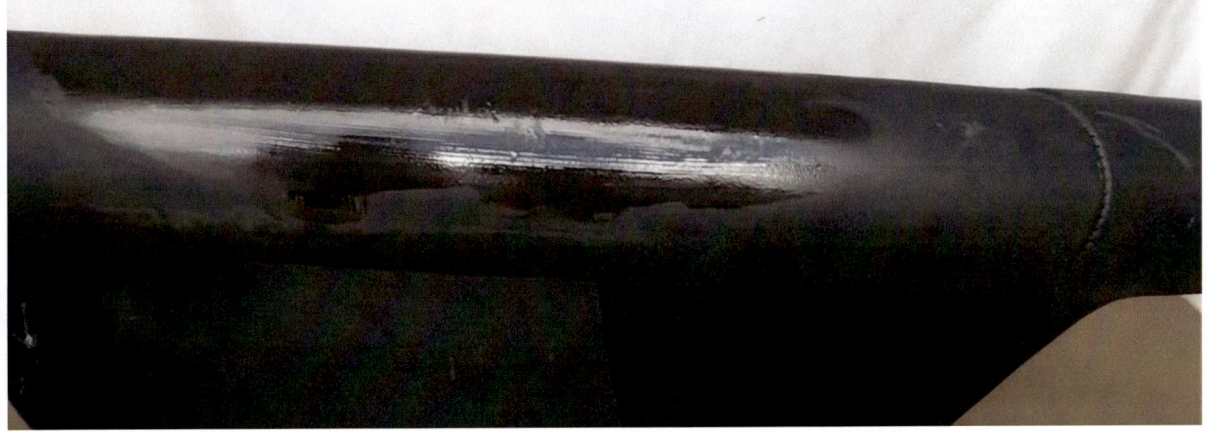
Color Testing

Step 6: Texturizing

- Use super glue and sandpaper to add texture to the repaired areas. Apply a thin layer of super glue over the paint and sand it gently to create a textured effect.

Step 7: Advanced Texturizing

- Optionally, apply a coat of Chip Guard, a bumper coater suitable for leather and vinyl, to enhance the texture and durability of the repaired areas.
- Ensure even application and avoid laying it on too thickly to maintain a fine mist finish.

Step 8: Spraying the Paint

- Load the custom color into a spray gun for a more straightforward application.
- Gently spray the paint over the repaired areas, ensuring even coverage and a seamless finish.
- Optionally, lightly sand the surface before spraying for better adhesion and finish.

Spray Paint

Restored Driving Wheel

7. Tips & Beginner Questions

20 Tips for Beginner Leather Restoration Projects

- **Start Small:** Begin with simple projects like repairing minor scratches or cleaning small leather items before tackling more significant projects.

- **Research:** Take the time to research different leather types, restoration techniques, and tools needed for your project.

- **Inspect Thoroughly:** Carefully examine the leather item for any damage or areas that need attention before starting the restoration process.

- **Test Products:** Always test cleaning and repair products on a small, inconspicuous leather area to ensure they don't cause damage.

- **Use Quality Products:** Invest in high-quality leather cleaning, conditioning, and repair products for the best results.

- **Follow Instructions:** Read and follow the manufacturer's instructions carefully when using leather care products.

- **Be Patient:** Leather restoration takes time and patience. Avoid rushing through the process to ensure a quality outcome.

- **Protect Surroundings:** Lay down protective materials to prevent surface damage while working on your project.

- **Work in a Well-Ventilated Area**: Ensure proper ventilation when using chemical-based products to avoid inhaling fumes.

- **Use Protective Gear:** Wear gloves and protective eyewear when handling harsh chemicals or using sharp tools

- **Clean First**: Always start the restoration process by thoroughly cleaning the leather to remove dirt, grime, and oils.

- **Condition Regularly**: Regularly keep leather soft and supple by applying a high-quality leather conditioner.

- **Avoid Direct Sunlight**: Store leather items away from direct sunlight to prevent fading and drying.

- **Address Stains Promptly**: Treat stains and spills on leather surfaces as soon as possible to prevent them from setting.

- **Be Gentle**: Handle leather items with care to avoid causing further damage during restoration.

- **Match Colors Carefully**: Choose leather dyes or paints that closely match the original color of the item for seamless repairs.

- **Blend Seamlessly:** Blend repaired areas with surrounding leather by feathering the edges and using light layers of dye or paint.

- **Let Products Dry Completely:** Allow leather cleaning agents, conditioners, dyes, and paints to dry thoroughly between applications.

- **Buff for Shine:** Use a soft cloth to buff leather surfaces after conditioning or applying polish for a smooth, shiny finish.

- **Seek Professional Help if Needed:** If you're unsure how to proceed or encounter significant damage, consider seeking assistance from a professional leather restoration expert.

Beginner Questions

Over the years, I have attended many physical/live classes on Leather Restoration. I always carry a diary and note common questions and suggested solutions.

Below are the most frequently asked questions, along with their suggested solutions. Please note that all solutions are suggested by various experts/participants. You can try them out and adopt the best one according to your results.

Question: What repair kits do you recommend for fixing cat scratches on leather furniture, and how can I address color loss when wiping down leather surfaces with a damp cloth?

Solutions Suggested:

- **Structural Damage Repair**: Structural damage on leather, such as scratches or flaps, requires a permanent solution for bonding the leather back together. Leather paint alone cannot achieve this. Instead, use a quality leather filler to fill the scratches and bond any flaps back in place. This ensures a lasting repair.

- **Ease of Repair**: Repair compounds offer an easier and faster solution than leather paint. With a repair compound, the scratches can be filled and bonded back in place within 15 minutes, providing a permanent fix. Mixing the color for the repair can be challenging for amateurs, but using a repair kit with premixed colors simplifies the process.

- **Application Technique:** When applying the repair compound, use two toothpicks - one as the leather glue applicator and the other dry.

Apply a small amount of glue to the top toothpick and place it underneath the areas with lifted flaps. Use a leather crack filler, a soldering iron, adjustable heat settings, and a copper-plated head for scratch areas. The heat from the iron melts the crack filler, allowing it to dissolve into the damaged areas and seal off the scratches effectively.

- **Finishing Steps**: Protecting the repaired areas is essential after applying the repair compound and crack filler. Apply a protective cream and use a hair dryer to dry it thoroughly. This ensures that the repaired areas are adequately protected and blended with the surrounding leather.

- **Product Recommendations**: Look for reputable brands such as LeatherMaster or other manufacturers that offer quality leather repair products. These products typically include everything needed for the repair process, including repair compounds, crack fillers, protective creams, and color-matching solutions.

- **Color Matching:** Achieving the right color match is crucial for a seamless repair. Take care to select the best color that matches the original leather to ensure a professional-looking result. Some repair kits come with pre-mixed colors, simplifying the color-matching process for DIY enthusiasts.

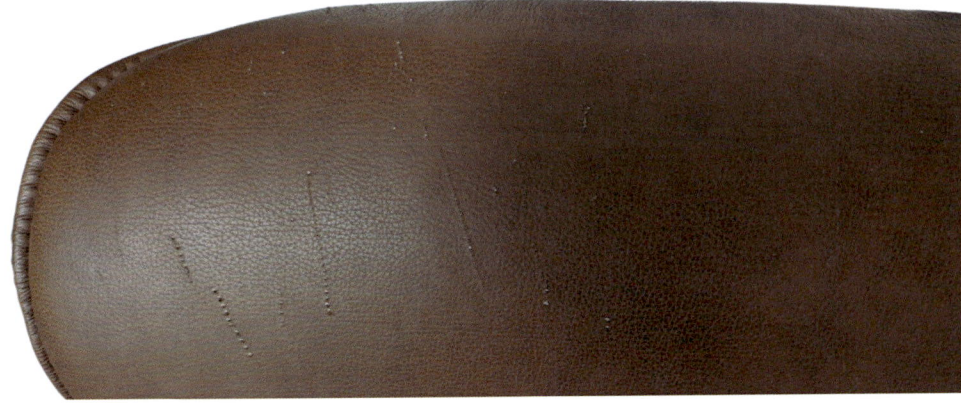

Cat Scratches

Question: I have recently dyed my leather couches dark brown, but unfortunately, the color didn't hold well. Can you provide assistance or guidance on how to address this issue?

Solutions Suggested:

- Proper prep work is crucial for any refinishing project, including leather restoration. Like a car body shop doesn't just paint over old paint, leather finishes require a specific process for permanent results. Quick-fix options may not provide lasting solutions, so it's essential to replicate the original leather finish for a durable outcome.

- Before attempting to refinish your leather furniture, it's essential to identify the current finish of the leather surface. Once identified, you must acquire the necessary products to replicate the original finish during restoration.

- The restoration process typically involves several steps, starting with deep cleaning to remove dirt and stains, followed by proper protection to prepare the leather surface. Next, applying a tack solution ensures proper adhesion between the clean surface and the dye substance, allowing for adequate drying time between applications.

- The chosen color is applied in multiple layers to achieve an even color distribution and blend faded or worn areas with non-blemished areas. Each layer requires sufficient drying time before proceeding to the next step.

- Purchase from a trusted vendor: Search for a supplier specializing in leather who can advise and recommend you based on your project.

- After applying the color, sealing coats are applied to protect the surface, followed by transparent dyes and additional solutions to enhance the finish and provide further protection. Allowing ample drying time between each application is crucial to ensure proper adhesion and drying.

- Finally, the refinished leather should be allowed to dry for several days before use, allowing all products to adhere and dry thoroughly. Following these steps diligently can help ensure a successful leather restoration project with long-lasting results.

Question: How can I tell if my leather is aniline or not?

- Understanding leather terminology and descriptions can be challenging for consumers, leading to confusion about leather types.

- Salespeople may only sometimes have the knowledge to describe leather types, adding to the confusion accurately.

- Manufacturers often use terms that may inflate the perceived quality of their products but need to be more easily understood by the general public.

- Consumers may look for a tag stating "aniline dyed" on their furniture when determining if the leather is aniline.

- However, having an "aniline dyed" tag does not necessarily mean the leather is pure aniline.

- The tag indicates the processes and materials used to achieve the leather's color, not its exact finish or manufacturing process.

- Many "aniline dyed" leathers may have a protective coating, such as polyurethane or silicone, applied to the finish.

- This protective coating, often called "Protected or Top Coated/Top Grained" leather, helps prevent staining and soiling.

- Additional resources, such as websites, can provide further information and clarification on identifying and understanding different types of leather.

Question: We want to restore this bed. We tried light tan balm on a small area, but we can still see marks even after a few coats. Then I tried a darker tan balm, but it was too dark. The light tan seemed the best match, but maybe because it's a balm, it will not cover marks well. Any suggestions on what is the best thing to do

- Light scratches on leather furniture can be fixed relatively easily.

- Based on your description and photos, there is no noticeable change despite using the light tan balm.

- "Balms" are typically ineffective and may not fully cover or repair marks. They're designed to pigment only the scratched area, not as a full refinishing product.

- Considering the need for results with the balm, it might be worth trying a different product of higher quality.

- If all else fails, refinishing the leather could be a permanent solution, albeit more involved than simply applying a product.

- The leather is an aniline wax pull-up hide, which can scuff or scratch more easily than pigmented leather.

- Suppose the darker area persists after using the balm. In that case, a solvent-based remover can help, but be aware that it may remove the additional problem and the original color.

- Proper maintenance of leather is essential to prevent drying out and damage from sunlight and temperature changes.

- For minor blemishes, a product like WaxOncan helps absorb the scratches, while more severe areas may require a filler.

- Alternatively, seeking assistance from a trained and certified leather repair technician can ensure the issue is handled correctly and effectively.

Question: We want to restore this bed. We tried light tan balm on a small area, but we can still see marks even after a few coats. Then I tried a darker tan balm, but it was too dark. The light tan seemed the best match, but maybe because it's a balm, it will not cover marks well. Any suggestions on what is the best thing to do

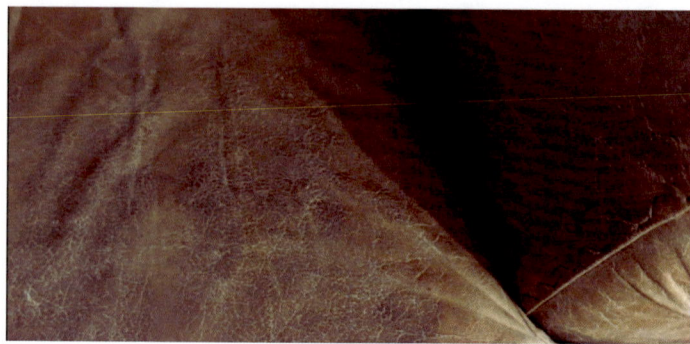

- If you have leather furniture with a wax oil pull-up aniline finish, you can restore it to its former glory with LeatherMaster's products. Their range can make it soft, supple, shiny, and rich in tone.

- Clean your furniture with Strong Cleaner to remove grime and stains. You may need a degreaser on the arms, seat cushions, and backrests close to the arms.

- After cleaning, use any product like/similar to LeatherMaster's Wax-On product to soften the leather and restore its shine. For blending and adhesion, you might need other products like color restore dye and tack-on products.

- Ensure thorough drying between each step using a hair dryer, and apply a sealer to coat over the dye, transparent aniline dye, protective cream, and finally, the wax-on finish. You should tackle one piece at a time for practicality and space utilization.

- Another option is to pinch and roll the leather during drying after applying the strong cleaner. This will open the leather cells and allow the protection cream to penetrate and address stubborn stains.

- If your leather is semi-aniline, it's soft but susceptible to staining and finish wear. A thorough cleaning and conditioning can significantly affect its appearance and condition.

Question: I accidentally applied too much oil to my old Hogan boots, resulting in dark stains on the right boot. Is there a way to remove these stains?

Based on your situation, the dark stains on your right boot resulted from applying too much oil. Here are some suggestions to address this issue:

- **Sun Exposure:** Try leaving the boots in the sun for several hours. The combination of heat and UV rays may help the oils to dry out, potentially lightening the stains over time.

- **Even Color**: Consider applying the same treatment to both boots to achieve uniformity in color. Unfortunately, it's unlikely that you'll be able to remove the stains from the leather altogether. The type of oil you used may have contributed to the problem. Many leather conditioners contain heavy animal fat oils like Neatsfoot oil, which can sometimes cause more harm than good.

- **Patience:** Ultimately, the best course of action may be to wait it out. Over time, the oils may evaporate, leading to a lightening of the stains. While this may not fully resolve the issue, it's a potential outcome to remember.

Keep in mind that the effectiveness of these methods may vary depending on factors such as the type of leather and the severity of the staining. It's always a good idea to spot-test any treatment on a small, inconspicuous area of the boots before proceeding with a complete application.

Question: After accidentally burning my leather couch with a BBQ lighter, I am seeking advice on how to fix it.

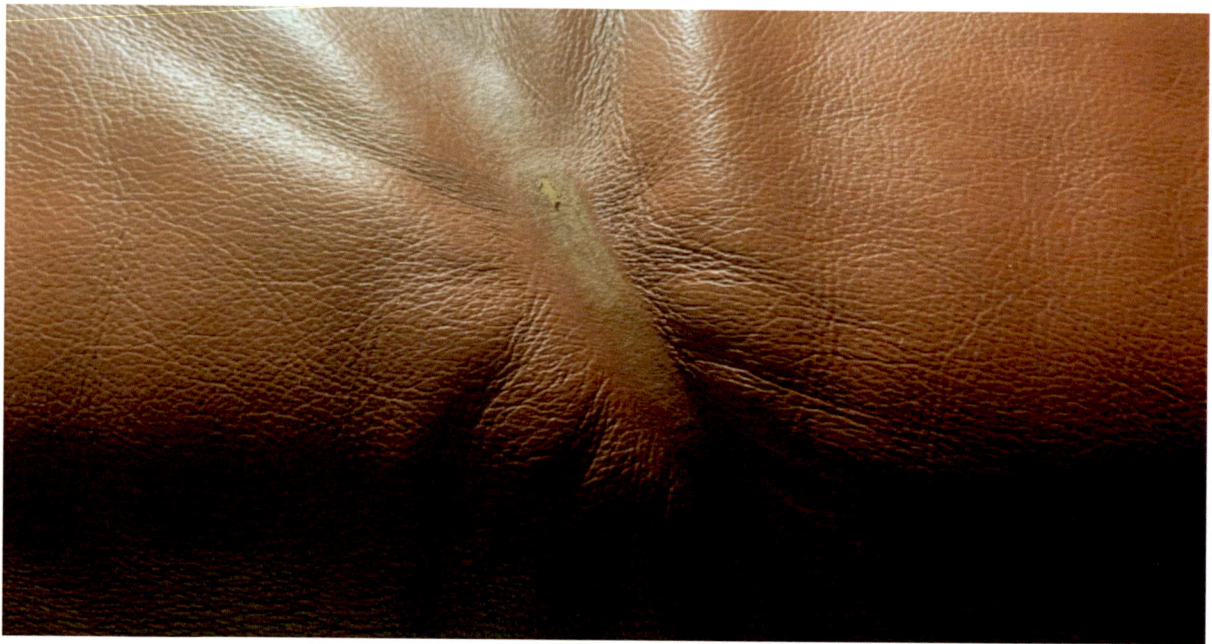

After accidentally burning your leather couch with a BBQ lighter, seeking advice on fixing it is understandable. Here are some comprehensive steps you can take to address the damage:

- **Assess the Damage:** Begin by thoroughly examining the extent of the damage caused by the burn. Determine the affected area and the severity of the burn marks.

- **Addressing Wrinkling**: The heat from the burn may have caused the leather to wrinkle and lose shape. One approach to tackling this issue is applying heat to the affected area. Start by spraying the wrinkled area heavily with plain water to moisten it. Then, immediately apply heat from a heat gun to the wet leather. Combining moisture and heat will help the leather relax; most wrinkles should disappear. It's crucial to keep the leather wet during the application of heat to prevent further damage or burning.

- **Consider Professional Assistance**: If the damage is extensive or the DIY methods don't yield satisfactory results, it might be best to seek professional assistance from a leather repair specialist. They have the expertise and specialized tools to handle various types of leather damage effectively.

- **Preventive Measures**: Once the damage has been addressed, consider implementing preventive measures to avoid similar incidents in the future. This may include placing protective covers or barriers around the leather furniture to minimize the risk of accidental burns.

- **Regular Maintenance**: Lastly, maintaining your leather furniture regularly can help prevent future damage and prolong its lifespan. This includes cleaning and conditioning the leather periodically using appropriate products recommended for your specific type of leather.

By following these steps, you can effectively address the damage caused by the burn and potentially restore the appearance of your leather couch. Always exercise caution and test any treatment on a small, inconspicuous area first to ensure compatibility and avoid further damage.

FAQ Table

Above were some specific questions that were asked by co-leathercrafters during live classes that I attended.

Additionally, there are some frequently asked questions (FAQs) that come up repeatedly on various forums. To make it easier, I've put together a table of 20 of these FAQs along with concise answers.

FAQS	ANSWERS
How can I tell if my leather is aniline?	Look for a tag stating "aniline dyed," but note it may not be pure aniline.
What should I do if my leather gets wet?	Wipe off excess water, let it air dry naturally, and condition afterwards.
How do I remove stains from leather?	Use a leather cleaner appropriate for the type of stain, followed by conditioning.
Can I repair scratches on leather?	Yes, small scratches can often be buffed out or filled with a leather repair kit.
What's the best way to condition leather?	Use a high-quality leather conditioner and apply sparingly in circular motions.
How do I prevent leather from cracking?	Regularly condition your leather and avoid exposing it to extreme temperatures.
Can I change the color of my leather?	Yes, you can dye leather with specialized leather dye products.
How do I protect leather from fading?	Keep leather away from direct sunlight and use UV protectant sprays or creams.
What's the difference between genuine and bonded leather?	Genuine leather is made from whole pieces of animal hide, while bonded leather is made from shredded leather scraps bonded together.
Can I repair a tear in leather?	Yes, tears in leather can be repaired using a leather repair kit or by a professional.

FAQS	ANSWERS
How do I remove unpleasant odors from leather?	Sprinkle baking soda on the leather, let it sit, then vacuum it off.
Can I use household products to clean leather?	It's best to use products specifically designed for leather cleaning.
How do I prevent mold and mildew on leather?	Store leather items in a dry, well-ventilated area away from moisture.
Can I restore cracked leather?	Yes, cracked leather can be restored with proper cleaning and conditioning.
Is it safe to use saddle soap on all leather?	Saddle soap is suitable for some leathers but may damage others.
What's the best way to store leather items?	Store leather items in a cool, dry place away from direct sunlight.
Can I use olive oil to condition leather?	While some people use olive oil, it's not recommended as it can go rancid over time.
How do I remove ink stains from leather?	Try rubbing alcohol or a specialized leather ink remover carefully.
Should I condition leather before or after cleaning?	It's generally recommended to condition leather after cleaning.
Can I use a hairdryer to dry wet leather?	It's best to let wet leather air dry naturally to avoid damaging it further.

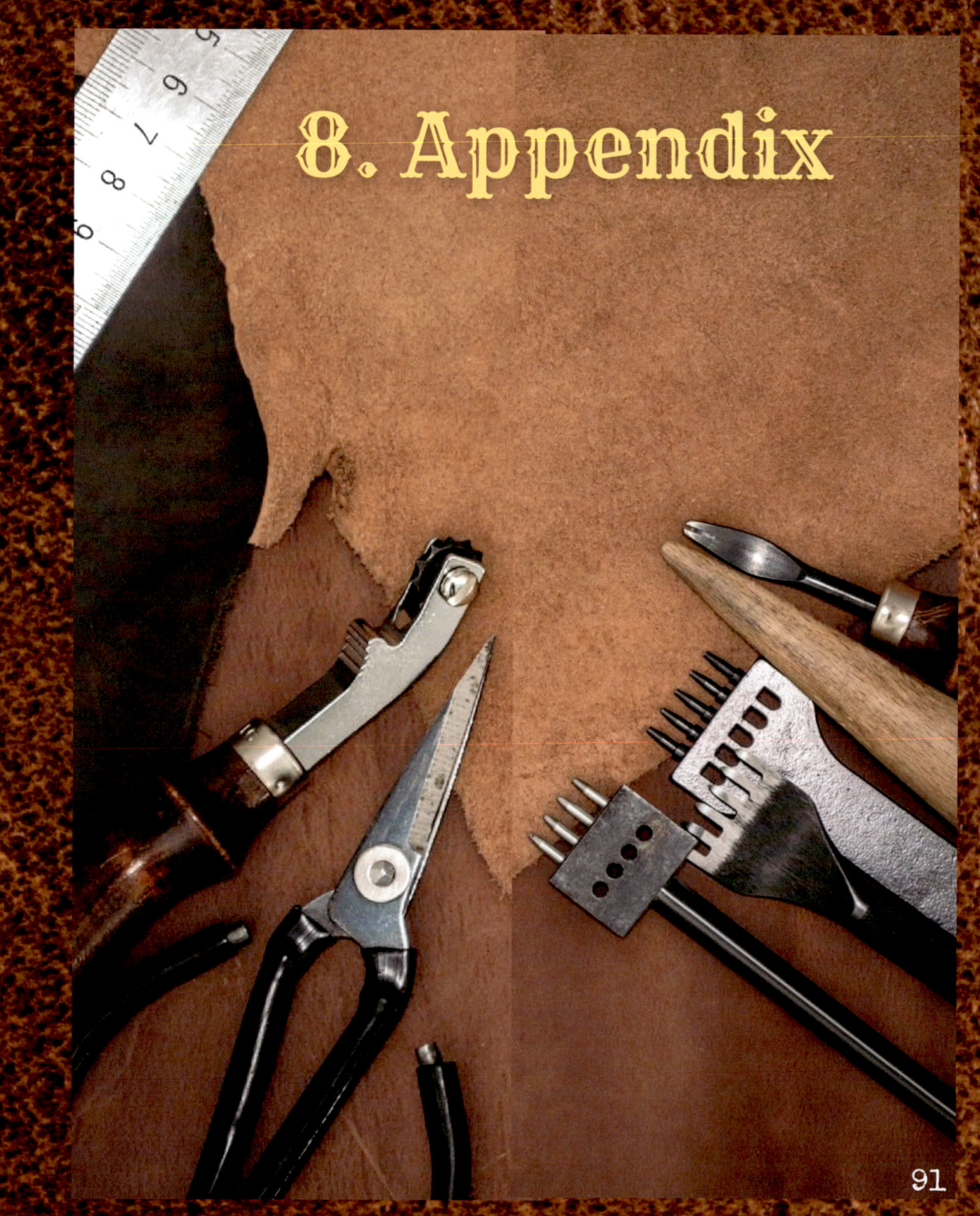

8. Appendix

APPENDIX 1 - LEATHER SUPPLIERS

Supplier Name	Website	Location
A & A CRACK & SONS LTD	www.aacrack.com	UK
A W NIDGLEY & SON LTD	www.awmidgley.co.uk	UK
ABBY ENGLAND	www.abbyengland.com	ENGLAND
ACADIA LEATHER	www.acadialeather.com	USA/ KY
AFRICAN GAME SKIN	www.africangameskin.co.UK	AFRICA
AMERICAN LEATHER DIRECT	www.aleatherd.com	USA/ KY
ARTISAN LEATHER	okwww.artisanleather.co.	UK
AVETCO LEATHER	www.avetcoinc.com	USA/ CA
BELTS PRODUCTION	www.beltsproduction.com	CROATIA
BRETTUNS VILLAGE	www.brettunsvillage.com	USA/ ME
BUCKLE GUY	www.buckleguy.com	USA/ MA
BUCKSKIN LEATHER	www.buckskinleather.com	CANADA
BUY LEATHER ONLINE	www.buyleatheronline.com	ITALY
DISTANT DRUMS	www.distantdrumsonline.com	USA / NY
DISTRIC LEATHERS	www.dublineleatherstore.com	IRELAND
DUBINE LEATHER STORE	www.fineleatherworking.com	USA/ CA

Supplier Name	Website	Location
FLETCHER	ukwww.fletcherhandmade.co.	UK
FROG JELLY LEATHER	www.frogjellyleather.com	USA/ TX
GEORDIE LEATHER	www.geordieleather.com	ENGLAND
GH LEATHERS	www.leathermerchants.com	ENGLAND
GOLIGER LEATHER	www.goligerleather.us	USA/ CA
HERMAN OAK LEATHER	http://www.hermannoakleather.com	USA/ MO
HIDE HOUSE	www.hidehouse.com	USA/ CA
IDENTITY LEATHERCRAFT	www.identityleathercraft.com	UK
ITAL LEATHER EXPERIENCE	www.italleatherexperience.com	ITALY
J. WOOD LEATHER LTD	www.jwoodleathers.co.uk	UK
LAEDERIET	www.laederiet.dk	DENMARK
LE PREVO	www.leprevo.co.uk	UK
LEATHER4CRAFT	www.leathercraft.co.uk	UK
LEATHER COSMOS	www.leathercosmos.com	GREECE
LEATHER CRAFT PATTERN	www.leathercraftpattern.com	HONG KONG
LEATHER DIRECT	www.leatherdirect.com.au	AUSTRAILIA

APPENDIX 2 - YOUTUBE CHANNELS FOR LEATHER RESTORATION PROJECTS

- James Berry - LeFrenchCrafter
- Insider Art
- LeatherRepairUK
- RubnRestore
- Leathertouchupdye
- geist.leathercare
- BedosLeatherworksLLC
- LeatherRepairEssex
- bagremake
- clydesleatherco
- LeatherTech Ireland
- Javier's Hobbies

APPENDIX 3 - ONLINE RESOURCES

Leather Craft Magazines

1. Shop Talk: https://shoptalk-magazine.com/

2. Leather Crafters Journal: https://leathercraftersjournal.com/

3. Euro Leather Norway: http://euroleather.no/

4. Russian Leather Crafting Magazine: http://www.en.leathercrafting-journal.ru/

5. Waxing the Thread U.K: https://gdhleathercourses.co.uk/

Free Downloadable Patterns

You can find free patterns for non-commercial and personal use on the sites below. Read the copyright document for each one carefully.

1. Leathercraft Pattern.com
2. Leathercove.com
3. Worldofpatterns.com
4. jlsleather.com

APPENDIX 4 - GLOSSARY

- **Aniline Leather:** Leather dyed exclusively with soluble dyes without any surface coating to preserve the natural appearance.

- **Burnishing:** Polishing leather edges to give them a smooth and glossy finish.

- **Conditioner:** Product applied to the leather to restore moisture, flexibility, and shine.

- **Cracks:** Splits or fractures in the leather surface caused by drying out or excessive stress.

- **Dye Transfer:** Transfer of color from one surface to another, often seen as stains on leather.

- **Edge Paint:** Colored or clear substance applied to the edges of leather to seal and finish them.

- **Patina:** Unique sheen or finish that develops on leather over time due to wear, handling, and exposure to oils.

- **Pigmented Leather:** Leather coated with a layer of pigment to provide color consistency and protection.

- **Restoration:** Repairing, refinishing, and rejuvenating leather to restore its original condition.

- **Scuff Marks**: Abrasions or scratches on the leather surface caused by friction or contact with rough surfaces.

- **Splits**: Under layers of leather separated from the surface layer, often used in lower-quality leather goods.

- **Stain:** Discoloration on leather caused by spills, dirt, or exposure to liquids.

- **Tooling:** Decorative process of creating designs or patterns on leather using specialized tools.

- **Vegetable Tanning:** Traditional method of tanning leather using natural tannins derived from plant materials.

- **Water Stains:** Marks or spots on leather caused by exposure to water, often resulting in discoloration or darkening.

- **Embossing:** Creating raised or sunken designs on leather by pressing it between patterned plates.

- **Fiebing's** is a well-known brand specializing in leather dyes, finishes, and care products.

- **Grain:** The surface texture of leather, determined by the natural markings and characteristics of the animal hide.

- **Horsehair Brush**: A brush made from horsehair is used for cleaning and polishing leather without scratching its surface.

- **Mink Oil:** Natural oil derived from mink fat, used as a leather conditioner and waterproof.

- **Neatsfoot Oil:** Oil extracted from the shinbones and feet of cattle, commonly used to condition leather.

- **Punching:** Process of creating holes or perforations in leather using a punch tool.

- **Skiving:** Thinning the edges of leather reduces bulk and creates smoother seams.

- **Stitching:** Joining pieces of leather together using stitches made with needles and thread.

- **Tack Cloth:** Cloth treated with a sticky substance to remove dust and particles from leather surfaces before finishing.

www.ingramcontent.com/pod-product-compliance
Lightning Source LLC
Chambersburg PA
CBRC091723070526
44585CB00008B/153